FANS
FIRST

FANS
FIRST

CHANGE THE GAME, BREAK THE RULES
& CREATE AN UNFORGETTABLE EXPERIENCE

JESSE COLE

LIONCREST
PUBLISHING

ANS FIRST

hange The Game, Break the Rules & Create

Unforgettable Experience

N   978-1-5445-2921-9   *Paperback*

978-1-5445-2922-6   *Ebook*

CONTENTS

WARNING!

This book might lead to gratuitous fun and the urge to Go Bananas. If you hate smiling, feeling good about yourself, feeling good about your fellow humans, banana puns, and generally having fun, then turn away now. This book is not for you. Also, you might be a grinch. Better look into that.

In Fans First style, Savannah Bananas fans were involved every step of the way in writing this book: choosing the title, selecting the cover, adding excerpts, and, most importantly, sharing their stories.

This book is for the fans and by the fans.

Part 1

CHANGE THE GAME

"If an organization is to meet the challenges of a changing world, it must be prepared to change everything about itself except its basic beliefs as it moves through corporate life...the only sacred cow in an organization should be its basic philosophy of doing business."

—JIM COLLINS AND JERRY I. PORRAS, *BUILT TO LAST*

Whatever's normal, do the exact opposite.

Here I go.

Hi! I'm Jesse Cole. I'll be your MC for this book. Why does this book have an MC? Well, this is not your typical book, and I am not your typical author. There will be some detours and asides. There will be some surprises and extras. There will be dad jokes and bathroom humor and goofy characters. There will also be bananas. Bunches and bunches of bananas.

Through all these detours, stories, and banana puns, you will learn a completely new way of doing business. The Fans First Way.

We'll get to what that means a little bit later. But first, a little about me. I'm the Yellow Tux Guy, author of *Find Your Yellow Tux*, speaker of keynotes, and owner of the world-famous Savannah Bananas baseball team.

In case you couldn't guess from my nickname and the name of my first book (or the cover of this one), I do own several yellow tuxedos—seven at the time this book was written (I may be the only repeat customer for brightcoloredtuxedos.com). I travel in my tux. I sleep in my tux. I speak in my tux. I even proposed to my wife in front of a sold-out crowd in my tux. Because I believe in standing out, my tux has become both my calling card and my uniform. When I'm in uniform, it can only mean one thing: it's showtime—time for me to have fun; time for my team to have fun; time for our fans to have the most fun of all.

I've been fortunate to share the Fans First Way on stages all over the world. Here in this book, I'm fortunate to share it with you. Just you and me together on this book adventure—me in my tux and you in your chaise lounge, your airplane seat, your hot tub... wherever you get your best reading in. Welcome to Bananaland.

March 26, 2021

THE PREGAME MARCH

"The show doesn't go on because it's ready. It goes on because it's 11:30."

—LORNE MICHAELS, SATURDAY NIGHT LIVE

It's five thirty. Game time isn't for another hour and a half. But game time isn't the same as showtime—and it's almost showtime.

I'm standing inside Hank Aaron Stadium in Mobile, Alabama, lined up with the team and ready for the Bananas March.

Now, when I say team, I don't just mean the baseball players. We've got a whole cast of characters I'd like you to meet.

First is the Bananas Pep Band, a group of musicians made up of high school band teachers, high schoolers, and college students—even drummers and saxophonists from rock bands.

Behind them are the Man-Nanas, the Bananas' dad-bod cheerleading squad. Filling their ranks (and stretching the limits of their clothes) are a rotating group of men ranging from their forties to seventies, each wearing cutoff shirts and short shorts that say "Just Peel It."

Next in line are our break-dancing first base coaches—two coaches who know very little about baseball but who sure can dance.

Behind them is our beloved mascot and the World's Strongest Banana, Split. Just look at those six-pack abs. That's the power of potassium, baby.

Finally, bringing up the rear, there is our baseball team—the Savannah Bananas. They're getting loose, but not in the traditional sense. Instead of warming up on the field, they are dancing in unison, ready to greet the fans.

Coming up at the end of the procession, there's me, decked out in my signature yellow tux and top hat. And for the first time ever before a Bananas game, I'm nervous.

We've done this pregame party hundreds of times before. But this time is different. This time, we're not warming up at our home ballpark at Grayson Stadium in Savannah, Georgia. We're hundreds of miles away in Mobile, Alabama. And tonight, we're kicking off the first (and only) leg of our inaugural One City World Tour.

That's why I'm nervous. We're in unfamiliar territory. We have no idea what's going to happen when we march through those gates. Will anyone show up for the pregame march? How will they react? Will they embrace the show, or will they be confused?

There are technical questions too. We've never put on a show at Hank Aaron Stadium before. We don't know how the sound is going to work. We barely know which gate to march through. We planned plenty, but we're still guessing about a lot of things and hoping it will all go right.

Still, everyone is fired up. The band is playing a little beat. The players are dancing back and forth, and the Man-Nanas are hooting and hollering like always. As I look around at everyone's energy and enthusiasm, a calm comes over me. It's going to be all right.

Just then, Zack, who is auditioning to join our entertainment team, hops on the microphone. "It's showtime!" he bellows.

And so it is.

The band strikes up its first song—the Mardi Gras classic, "You Move, You Lose"—and everyone starts clapping in unison. Just as we're ready to head out the gate, my phone rings. It's the mayor of Mobile. I answer the phone.

"I'm...Banana game. Do I...with...the...gate?"

"I'm sorry, Mr. Mayor. I can't hear you at all!" I say, trying to talk over the marching band right beside me.

"Oh...but...is that...hear...trumpets?"

"Mr. Mayor. Really, I'm very sorry. But I can't hear one word you're saying." Okay, maybe I could hear a few, but they didn't make any sense. "Just come to the ticket booth, and we'll help you there. I promise. I'm so sorry. But I have to go!"

I scramble to get my phone back in my pocket as the team sweeps me up and pushes me through the gate. As we round the corner, I see hundreds of fans lined up, and I breathe a sigh of relief.

Little Leaguers in full uniform come running up to high-five the players as other kids join in.

Moms and dads whip out their phones and start snapping pictures. The moms appear especially eager to get selfies with the Man-Nanas, who are bouncing around and shaking their pom-poms every which way they can.

The break-dancing first base coaches bust out some hot free-style moves.

The unicyclist starts weaving in and around the gathered crowd.

The band launches into another song, "Hey, Baby," and the entire cast starts waving their arms and singing in unison.

Me? I'm dancing around, too, soaking up the energy with every-one else.

Okay, well, I'm not dancing, really. That sounds way too grace-ful. What I'm doing is more like kicking and clapping along to the music. I turn to see a young toddler with a bow in her hair. She's smiling and clapping, thrilled with the circus all around her. I take her hand and invite her to dance with me.

I glance over to my left to see our players getting into the "Ooh, Ahh" hip thrust a little more than usual, and I just about lose it.

The song finishes, and then we kick into the final countdown. Starting from eleven (it's so boring to start from ten), the fans and cast count in unison.

11...10...9...8...7...6...5...4...3...2...1...showtime!

The fans cheer. The gates open, and the players make their way down the line, high-fiving every fan they can as they go. As the energy swells, the band launches into "Can't Stop the Peeling" (one of our Bananas traditions).

At this point, I realize I've lost track of the players. *They probably headed off the field to start warming up,* I think. Then I look over and see a player walking in from the parking lot. Then another. Then another. *Huh, that's strange. I wonder where they're coming from,* I think.

I look around the corner and see some more players off in the distance.

That's when I see it. The line.

Fans are wrapped around the entire parking lot waiting to get into the ballpark. The line is easily a quarter-mile long, almost to the side of the freeway. But everyone is beaming. Some are decked out in custom Bananas shirts and costumes. Many are carrying signs. Almost all of them are snapping photos, dancing along, and otherwise getting into the festivities.

I move up and down the line to greet them. Everyone tells me how excited they are to be here—and where they're from. We may be in Mobile, but fans have driven in from all over the country—from Chicago, from Baton Rouge, from Orlando, from Houston, from just about everywhere. They're ready for a show, and their energy is more than I could have imagined.

As I head back to the main gates, I lose myself singing the Banana Band's rendition of "Shut Up and Dance"—and then suddenly I realize I have to get down on the field. It's time for two of our mainstay pregame promotions: the First Banana and the Banana Baby.

I get to the field, look up at stands, and see the ballpark is absolutely packed with fans. A smile stretches out across my face, and it doesn't leave for the rest of the weekend.

I can't believe what we are about to do. A small independent-league baseball team from Savannah is now playing hundreds of miles away to sold-out crowds. The people of Mobile have literally never seen a Bananas show before, but they've already welcomed us with open arms.

How did this even happen? And what did the mayor want to talk to me about anyway?

That's what you're about to find out. Mostly. I never did find out what the mayor wanted, but I do know he saw a great show.

This is a book about how to be absolutely fanatical about creating fans.

The kind of fans who will sell out a show two nights in a row in a town you've never played in before.

The kind of fans who will show up two hours before the gates open to make sure they don't miss anything.

The kind of fans who create custom jerseys, shape their beards into bananas, and lead the crowd as part of an all-male cheerleading squad because the experience is that *good*.

Since 2016, the Savannah Bananas—an independent-league baseball team playing out of Savannah, Georgia—have operated by a single mission: Fans First, Entertain Always. Every decision we make, we ask if it's Fans First. If it's not, we don't do it.

The Fans First Way has been the key to the Bananas' success. It's how we've created a one-of-a-kind experience in a well-established industry. But here's the real secret: anyone in any business can do what the Bananas have done.

No, really.

You don't have to own a baseball team. You don't have to be in the entertainment industry. You don't even have to own a yellow tux.

A construction company in South Carolina can do it.

A small hotel in Southern California can do it.

A small film studio that started in Kansas City can do it.

These businesses all live in their own niches and serve different groups of people. But they all have one thing in common. They all believe that to create rabid, dedicated fans, all you have to do is change the game, break the rules, and create an unforgettable experience.

You're going to hear these companies' stories throughout the book, along with many of our own. Through these stories, we're going to teach you the Fans First Way. But first, to truly understand the Fans First Fanomenon, we need to start all the way back at the beginning—back at a time when our new Savannah ballclub had no money, no name, and no guarantees that our grand experiment would work out.

START BEFORE YOU ARE READY

"The secret to getting ahead is getting started."

—MARK TWAIN

Grayson Stadium was empty.

There was no equipment. The phone and internet lines had been cut. The office (if you could even call it that) was bare. Outside of a plastic folding table that we found in a storage room, there was no furniture anywhere.

And it smelled. Really bad. Maybe it was the dirty, ripped carpets tossed about everywhere. Maybe it was all the water damage throughout the stadium. Maybe it was the bitter ghosts of baseball teams past, attacking our nostrils in hopes of scaring us away.

Whatever it was, it wasn't pleasant.

Still, it was Grayson Stadium. *Historic* Grayson Stadium. A classic, old-school ballpark that had been standing proudly in Savannah since 1926. A place with a story, a richness, and a character that couldn't be ignored.

Babe Ruth played there. Hank Aaron played there. Tons of other greats played there, too, as they worked through the minor leagues on their way to the Big Show. But for some reason, none of the other teams that played in Savannah could ever draw a crowd. Sure, some had been more popular than others, but the story always ended the same for every team: they failed to engage the city; the city got tired of them, and they left for greener pastures (or they folded entirely).

I saw this for myself in 2014, when my wife and Fans First Entertainment co-founder Emily surprised me with a trip to Savannah. We arrived at Grayson Stadium on a perfect eighty-degree night to watch the former team play. As we walked through the huge brick walls at the front gate, I looked at Emily and said, "This ballpark is magical."

But apparently, we were the only ones who knew it. About a hundred people sat scattered about in a 4,000-person ballpark. The players played. The fans sat and watched. And that was about it. Even the music playing over the speakers between innings sounded bored.

What had happened here? How could such a great ballpark in such an amazing town be so lifeless? I'd heard Savannah was well-known for its ghosts, but I didn't expect Grayson to be a literal ghost town.

Later, we did some digging. The current team was on the outs with the city. The problem? Grayson Stadium. It was too old. It needed too many repairs. It needed to go away so the team could build a brand-new $38 million stadium.

The city balked at the idea. It saw the team's demands for exactly what they were. The team thought a shiny new object could fix all their problems. The city saw a ballclub that could barely draw a hundred people to a game. If no one was going to come, what did it matter where they played?

Besides, there was nothing wrong with Grayson. It just needed a little love. Smelling an opportunity (or maybe that was the water damage), I texted the commissioner of the Coastal Plain League: "If this team ever leaves, I want to come here."

Lo and behold, the team left after the next season. Here was our shot to bring a new brand of baseball to Savannah.

Flash forward a year later, and it was move-in day. Grayson was old, smelly, and empty, and we had a ton of work to do. So we pulled out the folding table from storage, sat down, and got cracking.

Sitting at the table were me, my wife Emily, our twenty-four-year-old president Jared Orton, and three twenty-two-year-olds straight out of college, including Marie Matzinger, who is now our Fans First Director. On day one, our first order of business was simple: get on the phone and reach out to as many people in the community as possible.

After a few calls, a pattern started to emerge:

"Wait. Who are you?" the person on the other end of the line would say.

"We're Savannah's new baseball club!"

"Oh yeah? What big league team do you represent?"

"Actually, we're an independent-league baseball team." We didn't say we were a college summer baseball team. We were too embarrassed.

"Uh-huh..."

Silence.

"Anyway, we were wondering if we could set up a meeting with you to see if you would be interested in partnering with us this season or helping us get the word out."

"No thanks."

Click.

Occasionally, we would actually score a meeting, but when we showed up, we were practically laughed out of the room. Prospective sponsors would hear our pitch, pat us on the back, and say, "Good luck." Then, they'd show us the door.

They said, "Good luck," but what they really meant was, "You kids don't stand a chance, and I don't want anything to do with you."

Even the sports bar right outside the stadium was skeptical. Knowing they had been a huge booster for the previous team, we headed over to introduce ourselves to our new neighbor. Our welcome was frostier than the beer.

"I heard you won't be serving alcohol," the bar owner said.

"No, we will definitely be serving alcoholic beverages," I said. "We were even thinking you could be our partner."

"Well, I heard you aren't going to, so no."

Great. Not only were we battling indifference, but we were also battling misinformation.

I'll be honest. Getting rejected over and over again sucked. But we were young, excited, and convinced that if we kept showing up, if we kept getting in front of people, then eventually things would break in our direction.

To help move that process along, in November we decided to throw a big launch party. We rented out a conference center, hired a fancy caterer, and invited as many people as we could.

Only eighty people showed up, a lot of them local press.

I had my yellow tux, but it was in the closet. I was too scared to wear it. I was afraid to stand out. As the new kids in town, we were trying to fit in.

We announced our Name the Team contest and invited the entire city to participate. We had season tickets available. We sold two.

When no one's heard about you, when you don't stand out, no amount of free crab cakes or fancy cocktails can draw people to your party.

It wasn't just that people weren't interested in us. They actually felt bad for us—the caterers never even sent us a bill for the event! Then, when we asked them if they were interested in running the food and beverage operation at our games and offered them a big cut of the money, they turned us down flat. No negotiations. No questions. Nothing.

From October 2015 to January 2016, we worked tirelessly to connect with the community—with partners, press, and fans. We marketed the team through newspaper and radio ads and posted on social media. No one was interested. The city's message was unmistakable: no baseball team had ever made it in Savannah before. Why should we be any different?

It was a fair question. One we couldn't answer.

Because we *weren't* any different. We were acting like everyone else. We were talking instead of showing. We were advertising and marketing and selling by the normal rules.

We were chasing customers, not creating fans.

All we knew at the time was that if we didn't turn things around soon, this whole venture was going to be over before it started.

A couple of years after Southwest Airlines was founded, a reporter asked founder Herb Kelleher what his business strategy was. "It's called doing things," he said.

Obviously, his answer was tongue-in-cheek, but the idea also has merit. So many of us overthink. We tinker with our business strategy behind closed doors like mad scientists, trying to make our creation perfect before we reveal it to the world. But here's the rub: it's never perfect. A better strategy is to start before you are ready. Do, so you can learn. You won't know anything until you put yourself in front of potential fans.

The brilliant philosopher Mike Tyson famously said, "Everyone has a plan until they get punched in the face." When we started, we got hit pretty hard by the response from the community. Instead of making excuses, we made ourselves different.

The only way to win in business is to make adjustments, not excuses.

CONSTRAINTS FOSTER CREATIVITY

"You can't build a reputation on what you're going to do."

—HENRY FORD

"Jesse, this is Alex. We're out of money, and we're not going to be able to make payroll this week."

I almost spit out my drink.

No one ever wants to get that message. Especially not when you're at your best friend's wedding.

We couldn't hide from the facts either. Our fledgling ballclub had no money left, and we still had over five months to go until opening day.

But we weren't ready to call it quits just yet.

Emily and I sat in silence for most of the ride home, each of us trying to process the situation we were in. Finally, she turned to me and said, "We're going to have to sell the house."

She was right. We were also going to have to empty our savings accounts and sell anything else we could. And that's exactly what we did.

Just like that, we were all-in. Our fate was our team's fate. No looking back.

We didn't sleep much over the next few months. Partly because of the air mattress. Partly because of the cockroaches that found their way into our rundown duplex. But mostly because we had a lot on our minds.

Instead, Emily and I took a lot of midnight walks. On the moonlit streets of Tybee Island, we talked about everything and anything on our minds—the launch, hiring, design, revenue strategies, media requests, you name it. Since we couldn't afford to hire any staff, we had to manage everything ourselves.

Still, the team members we did have were bonafide all-stars. First, there was our president, Jared. Sure, he was only twenty-four, but there was a reason we trusted him with the big job. I had first met him a few years earlier when he was working as an intern for my previous ballclub. Right away, I could see that he was smart, passionate, and a born leader. So when an opportunity opened up in Savannah, he was the only person we wanted to help us run the show.

He didn't take much convincing. He'd always wanted to launch a team of his own, and he shared our vision for a one-of-a-kind baseball experience. As Jared put it, "I had fallen in love with how Jesse and Emily saw and did things, what they did for people, and how they thought differently."

Just like Emily and me, Jared was all-in on making this team work. He had left a job as assistant general manager for the Burlington Royals just so he could take his chances with us, and his whole baseball career was riding on our success.

So when the money ran out, naturally, he began to wonder if he'd made the right choice. Was he in over his head? Would he be able to live up to the expectations he had set for himself? Would we be able to save baseball in Savannah?

Darn right we would.

Yes, it was an uncertain time for all of us. But it was also a time of excitement and energy. Without a safety net and eager to bring a new brand of baseball to Savannah, we were going to have to get creative.

The next several months were a blur, but a happy one. Emily, Jared, Marie, and I were eating, sleeping, breathing our new ball-club 24/7. Failure was staring us in the face, but to us, success was inevitable. As Emily likes to say, we were so high on life and so sure that if we just tried hard enough, we could make it work.

Enter our secret weapon: our willingness to try anything. We'd already tried the normal stuff, and it had failed. We'd have to do things differently. Be different.

We all had experience in the baseball world already. We'd even seen a good amount of success. But none of us had ever built a team from scratch—and certainly not in the way we were planning to do it. There weren't any rules for what we were trying to do, which gave us the freedom to make things up to see what worked.

Driving this effort was Fans First Director Marie Matzinger. As she put it, joining the team right out of college, Marie didn't know that we did things differently from other teams. She didn't have to deprogram from the business-as-usual approach that other organizations took. If she thought something might point us in the right direction, she shared her idea, and we tried it.

And if something didn't work? All good. We learned our lesson and then showed up the next day ready to try something else.

Most importantly, we never got down on each other. It's critical to let people know you have their back and that you care for them. Our fate was uncertain, and we were stretched nearly beyond our limits, but we believed in each other—and we poured that belief back into the team. Ultimately, it was that blind optimism that helped us break through.

Constraints foster creativity. If we'd had money pouring in and plenty of resources, we might have been tempted to go with the status quo. With no money, we had to go with the capital we did have: each other. We had to outthink, not outspend. We couldn't afford to be like every other team—and we were losing by trying to be. We had to go big and go different.

Years after our launch, we still look at constraints as an opportunity that pushes us to do things we've never done. Most teams have a sound person and a PA announcer. During the course of a normal ballgame, there's plenty to do for two people. But we don't have two people. We just have the Shark. And the Shark embraces his constraints.

Mark "The Shark" Ediss has been with us since day one and is the best in the business. Even before we had a team name, Shark was reaching out to be a part of the Bananas. At his audition, he actually sang and played music just to show us he could bring the energy. I told him he got the job, but there was one rule: no dead air.

Shark never breaks that rule. He does everything—announcing, music, sound effects. It's a two-hour marathon of energy. He doesn't stop until the last fan leaves. After a game, he looks like he went fifteen rounds with Floyd Mayweather, sweating with a towel around his neck. He's so good at filling the show with energy that if all of a sudden there was dead air during a show, we'd be rushing to the booth to make sure Shark hadn't keeled over.

Even if Shark is sometimes off his game, he still doesn't miss a beat. During the first game of our One City World Tour, for instance, Shark was supposed to kick the game off with the National Anthem. Instead, Shark cued up the seventh-inning-stretch classic "Take Me Out to the Ballgame."

"A-one, a-two, a-one, two, three, four," Shark said and then launched into the first line of the song.

"Nope. National Anthem, Shark," I said, jumping onto the mic to cut him off.

Everyone in the stadium broke out in laughter.

Shark laughed along and did a quick pivot, and moments later, everyone was singing along.

That's how Shark rolls. Where others might bury their heads from embarrassment, Shark embraced the moment and created a Fans First experience even out of a little flub.

Shark has become such a leader in moments like this that he's impossible to replace. So we don't even try.

Later during the 2021 season, Shark had to miss a game. Instead of bringing in another PA announcer, we asked, "What could we do if we didn't have an announcer?" We got creative. We had kids in the crowd introduce players. We had a hype person walk players up to bat to introduce them. We had teammates introduce each other. After watching a few teammates have fun with each other, we asked, "What if a player introduced himself coming to bat?" Bill LeRoy was all over it. He walked up to the plate, microphone in hand. Then he bellowed, "Now coming to bat, number one, University of North Georgia Alum, myself!" Then he threw the mic into the dugout. The moment went viral, generating millions of views on social media and even being featured on ESPN.

If we had avoided constraints rather than embraced them, moments like this never would have happened.

ATTENTION BEATS MARKETING

*"I can accept failure; everyone fails at something.
But I can't accept not trying."*

—MICHAEL JORDAN

In my office, there is a custom poster of PT Barnum plastered with the quote, "Without promotion something terrible happens...nothing!"

From the moment he opened his American Museum in New York, Barnum was always looking for new ways to generate attention. He put flags on the roof of his museum that could be seen a mile away. He built a wraparound balcony and had bad musicians play on it. He installed a huge revolving lamp on the roof—the first spotlight. He hung huge color paintings of animals and oversized banners on the outside, including one of a man playing violin backward. He ordered a magnificent carriage shaped like an English walnut for Commodore Nutt. He brought Jumbo the elephant and the first live hippopotamuses to America.

According to author Joe Vitale in his book *There's a Customer Born Every Minute*, PT Barnum's number-one rule was "Get Attention." And boy did he follow that rule to the letter.

With the people of Savannah all but ignoring us, we needed attention—and we needed it bad. Turning to the Greatest Showman to find inspiration, we asked ourselves one question: "What would PT Barnum do?"

We didn't have money for an elephant or musicians (even bad ones), but we knew we could find other ways to get our fans involved with the team and start to generate attention. After all, constraints foster creativity. We had to reinvent the way we got the word out. We had to break the rules of advertising and marketing.

So we announced our Name the Team contest.

But we knew that was just the start. If we could land on a good team name, then we could really get future fans engaged.

The idea worked. Our Name the Team contest was the only good thing to come out of our launch party back in November. The local press ate the story up (along with a few crab cakes), and the papers ran with it the next day.

Finally, we had a little attention.

The suggestions started coming in soon after. They ranged from the absurd (the Savannah Baseball McBaseballface) to nods to local lore (the Savannah Ghosts). Some of the suggestions were pretty good, but none of them stood out. None of them felt like *us*.

Except one. Actually, it was one of the first suggestions we got, submitted by a future fan named Lynn Moses: the Savannah Bananas.

That was our winner. That was a name with appeal.

How did we know it was the right name for us? Well, say it out loud. Listen to how it rolls off the tongue. It just has a certain ring to it.

More than that, Savannah Bananas was the only idea that gave us more ideas. The second we heard it, we started thinking about all the other promotions we could run with a name like that. The First Banana. Banana in the Pants. The Banana Nanas. The Banana-shaped tickets. (Don't worry, I'll explain what all those things are later.) The name was full of possibilities, and we were sold on it almost immediately.

Now we just had to rally the people of Savannah around it.

This wasn't going to be easy. If the past few months had made one thing clear, it was that the people of Savannah were already indifferent to hostile about our existence. Naming our team after a fruit—and not even a local fruit—was going to feel rotten to some people.

It certainly did to Savannah's director of park services. Not long before our big unveiling, he came up to me and said, "So I hear you're going to name your team the Bananas."

"Where did you hear that?" I deadpanned.

"Some of my staff found out that you trademarked the name," he said.

I smiled and shrugged.

"Good luck with that," he said. Then he walked off.

We knew we were taking a risk with the name, but we weren't going to let anyone's reactions catch us flat-footed. This time, we were going to engineer the narrative and take our destiny into our own hands.

To do this, we did two things. First, we began coaching our staff on how to respond to the inevitable criticism. We couldn't control the response, but we *could* control how we responded to it. We could even have a little bit of fun in the process.

Second, we brought in ringers. When we announced the name during the big unveiling ceremony, we'd have a guaranteed cheering section. In the weeks leading up to the announcement, I had this recurring nightmare that we'd announce the name and no one would do anything. No cheering, no booing. Just silence.

No way I was going to let that happen. Criticism I could handle, but not indifference. If that meant rounding up a group of energetic folks to go completely bananas when we announced our name, then it would only add to the experience of our big announcement ceremony.

Soon, the big unveiling was upon us, and everything went exactly as planned. Actually, better. We even caught the attention of some national sports press, with the people at *SportsCenter* dubbing us "top banana" and calling our design logo of the year. Meanwhile, our merchandise started selling all across the country—and even across the world.

The sudden boost in merch sales especially caught us by surprise. We had to learn a lot about shipping logistics in a short amount of time. And don't even get me started on international shipping costs. Who knew that it cost so much more to send a box of shirts to Australia than it did to send them to Alabama? We didn't—but we sure knew now.

We also learned the importance of a reliable supply chain. By the time the orders started rolling in, we still hadn't received any hats from our supplier. All we had to sell were our T-shirts—and they spelled our name wrong. As funny as it might be, we couldn't sell "Banannas" shirts. That would *not* make a very good first impression! (Side note: I'm pretty sure we still have those shirts in storage somewhere. Maybe one day we'll run a bad shirt giveaway so our fans can own a piece of history.)

As good as the reaction was on the international stage, things weren't looking as rosy back home. The press savaged us, and the locals were embarrassed by our choice. Here is just a sampling of the feedback we received:

> The single most ridiculous, insulting, hideous, embarrassing, outlandish name for a baseball team. You'll be giving away tickets so you can keep the morale of your team going.

This is an embarrassment to the city of Savannah. How redneck can you be?

The owner doesn't know anything about baseball. Pathetic name and organization.

Whoever came up with the name should be fired and ridden out of town on a rail.

Bananas, that's the stupidest name ever for a baseball team. I will never attend a game or go to Grayson Stadium until the name is changed. Boooooooo.

They never gone win with a name like that.

We were the laughingstock of the community. But while the criticism stung a little, once again we looked to the wisdom of the Greatest Showman. "You know," PT Barnum once said, "I'd rather be laughed at than not be noticed at all."

Besides, in our eyes, we'd won the conversation. We finally had Savannah's attention. People were talking about us. They were equal parts confused and curious, irritated and interested. They knew we represented a different kind of baseball team, even if they didn't know exactly what that meant yet.

Now that we had their attention, all we had to do was keep the pressure on. A bunch of other announcements followed:

- Our tickets would be all you can eat. All your burgers, hot dogs, chicken sandwiches, chips, soda, water, and dessert for $15.

- On social media, we unveiled sports' first senior citizen dance team, the Banana Nanas.

- At a local elementary school, we unveiled our mascot Split, the Prince of Potassium. Why an elementary school? We figured a crowd of adults would be split on Split, but that the kids would embrace him. Which they did—swamping him with hugs.

- As the 2016 election got underway, we offered outgoing president Barack Obama an internship with our organization. (He didn't accept. But he did accept Spotify's offer to become President of Playlists, which I admit was probably the better offer.)

With each new event, we ratcheted up the attention and taught people who we were. Slowly, the mistruths that had been flying around about us started to fade away. No longer were we the buzzkills who refused to serve alcohol at our games. From now on, we were the buzzworthy rule-breakers ready to light up the city. We were here to play, and we were here to stay.

More importantly, we'd finally cracked the code on how to get the city's attention. Savannah had dismissed all their previous teams for being just like most baseball teams—long, slow, and boring. When we first arrived in the fall of 2015, we played it too safe. It was only natural that people would assume we were long, slow, and boring too.

We couldn't go after Savannah's hearts until we had their eyes and ears. We understood that now. The naming contest got the city's attention, and we were relentless in our approach in the months that followed. Eventually, that attention led to ticket sales, which led to our first sellout. And then our second. And then our third.

Now that we knew we'd have fans in the seats, there was only one thing left to do: execute.

EVERY GAME IS SOMEONE'S FIRST

"Success is on the other side of 'You can't do this.'"

—JAMES ALTUCHER

We sold out opening night.

I know. Even all these years later, I'm still just as surprised as you are.

Unfortunately, opening night was no victory lap.

Problem number one: the all-inclusive ticket. With the Bananas, we wanted to create a one-of-a-kind stadium experience. Our tickets not only get you admission into the ballpark, but all the food you can eat at our concessions stands.

No team had ever done that before—including us and our team of twenty-somethings and interns.

It was a big risk, but we were determined to make it work. So in the hours before we opened the gates, it was all hands on deck getting the food ready, making sure all the napkins and condiments were stocked, and training everyone up.

Then the rain hit. Hello, problem number two.

It was four o'clock. We weren't set to open the gates for another hour. But that didn't matter to the fans. The second it started pouring, everyone who had showed up early rushed to the stadium to get out of the rain. We didn't even think about trying to stop them. Really, we couldn't—we didn't have any barriers up!

As the concourse filled with people, we looked at each other, bewildered. "All right," someone finally said, "guess we'll try to open."

Suddenly, we had a full concourse of people—very, very hungry people. We weren't even close to being ready, and the demand quickly overwhelmed us. Some people waited as long as two hours before they finally got to eat.

Meanwhile, the rain kept coming. A lot of it. Our brand-new fans weren't only cold, wet, and hungry; they were also bored.

That was where I drew the line. *No one* gets bored in Bananaland. Not on my watch.

The best opportunity to do the unexpected and create a fan is when something goes wrong.

So I walked up to the Banana Nanas. "Um, can you go out and dance in the rain?"

They stood there for a moment, staring at me in their white jerseys like I was crazy. Then they nodded, and one of them said, "All right, let's do it!"

A few minutes later, the Nanas were out in front of the tarp, dancing like there was no tomorrow. The fans got into it, singing along, taking videos, and laughing and smiling with the Nanas.

Finally, at around 8:30, the rain stopped, and we could get on with the game.

I headed down to the field and loaded up onto the trolley with the rest of the players. (Yes, a trolley. We thought it would be a fun way to make our grand entrance.) As the trolley reached the field, I looked up at the crowd to see if anyone was still in the stands.

They were full. Not a single person had left. Rain or shine, they were here for the show.

Then, the Bananas put on an amazing, lights-out performance, blanking the opposing team and basking in their first dominant win of the season.

Or not. The Bananas stunk—big time. They could barely even hold the ball, making six errors on their way to an epic loss.

It was a good thing we wore our green uniforms that day because we weren't quite ripe yet.

We didn't win on the field. We didn't start on time. We couldn't keep our fans dry. We couldn't feed them the way we would have liked. We couldn't even put on the show we'd planned.

But somehow, in some way, we connected with our fans. Grayson Stadium was as full after the final out as it was for the first pitch—I mean, the first *banana*.

I'm still not entirely sure how we did it. If there's a word that somehow splits the difference between *cursed* and *magical*, that would be the one I'd use to describe opening night.

Ultimately, that's the power of doing and learning. You can talk until you're blue in the face about what to do, but until you're in the middle of it and actually executing, you won't have the full picture. It wasn't until we had four thousand wet, hungry people begging for burgers and hot dogs that we truly understood how much food we needed to make—and when we had to start making it.

Besides, as embarrassing as some of our miscues were, we weren't in this for just one game. We were in it for the long haul.

When Disneyland opened on July 17, 1955, it was a disaster.

Half the rides didn't work. The asphalt hadn't set on Main Street, and women's heels got stuck in the heat. The plumbing in the bathrooms didn't work, and people relieved themselves wherever they chose. The park was well over capacity, with a lot of people hopping fences to get in. The opening was so bad that the day will forever be known in Disney lore as "Black Sunday."

But here's the thing: When people think about Disneyland today, they don't think about those rocky first months. In fact, most people don't even know about Black Sunday and all the course corrections that followed. Instead, they think of Disneyland as the Happiest Place on Earth, a place full of rides and wonders that has thrilled the world for decades.

Bananaland might not operate on the same scale as Disneyland, but we were banking on a similar effect. If we could connect with our new fans, if we could show them what we stood for and what we were trying to build, they would forgive us for a few hiccups along the way.

Luckily, we were able to create that connection. One moment from that night will always stand out to me above all the others, a moment that revealed not only the tremendous opportunity we had to connect with this community but also the tremendous responsibility we had to live up to our promise: Fans First, Entertain Always.

During the game, a young woman approached me and said, "Excuse me. Is it possible to get a signed baseball?"

I smiled. "Sure! I'll see what we can do."

I asked her what brought her out to the ballpark. She said she was there on behalf of her fiancé, who had recently passed away. A lifelong local, he had come to every opening night at Grayson Stadium since he was a kid. She had come to the game with his family in his honor. "If there's any way to get a baseball, it would mean a lot to all of us," she said.

I was stunned. "Of course we'll get you a ball," I said.

"One more thing," she said. "My fiancé's name was Drew Moody, and I noticed you also have a player on your roster with the same name. Could you make sure he signs it?"

I explained to her that Drew wasn't with us yet because he was still finishing up his baseball season in college. But his younger brother Logan was also on the team, and he was already here. I promised I would talk to him.

Quickly I tracked Logan down and told him the story.

He nodded. "Give me the ball," he said. Then, I watched as he tracked down every single player and had them sign it.

Then, he walked up to the bleachers, introduced himself, and sat down next to her. For a full half-inning, the two sat and talked together like they were old friends.

Then, he stood up, handed her the ball, gave her a big hug, and walked off.

"Wow, Logan," I said when I saw him later.

"Fans First, right?" he said.

Right.

Every game is someone's first game. This is something both Emily and Jared have said since day one. Logan Moody provided a special moment for that young woman at her first game—our first game. And it was in that moment that I truly understood the power of first impressions—no matter the obstacles.

When adversity hits, most people dwell on the negative. It's raining. We've lost power. There's construction. There are traffic delays. The AC went out. The refrigerator stopped running. They don't have a plan B. They're controlled by this obstacle the world put in front of them.

When things go wrong, when there's a challenge with the experience, that is the best time to wow your fans. They're not expecting you to make a random wrong a right. It's a little heroic. Or, as Bananas catcher Bill LeRoy might say, a little joyful.

"Happiness is by chance. It's situational," he says, citing a sermon he once attended. "Happiness is sunny weather and walk-off home runs on fireworks night. That makes you happy. Then you come to a Bananas game, and it gets rained out. That's a situation that didn't go your way. But it's now your new situation. Instead of letting that affect you and choosing to be upset, you choose joy instead."

That's what Fans First is. No matter what's going on or how bad things are going, you can always choose joy instead of waiting for happiness to come along.

How you view things
is how you do things.

Setbacks happen, whether it's rain or something else. It could be a perfect night for a ballgame, and the visiting team could get a flat tire and not arrive at the stadium until 8:45. The power could go out in the middle of a game. A bull could get loose from the bullpen (that's why they call it that, right?).

Those are the kinds of delays that tend to happen to us, but every business has its own version of this situation. Instead of getting caught flat-footed, why not have a script so you can keep entertaining your fans?

After opening day, we learned that even when it rains, we can still provide everything else that makes Bananaland so special—the player connections, the promotions, the character acts, the pep band, all of it. Just add water. We've learned to turn adversity into opportunities to create Fans First moments—both for the fans and for us. It's one of the things that makes us so fanatical about our fans.

Now think about your own business. How do your fans feel? Is your experience remarkable? If not, what can you do to treat every interaction like it's the *first* one?

Dig in. Script around the obstacles. Eliminate friction. Entertain. Engage. Empower. Go all-in on what you stand for and what makes you different.

Be a fanatic. That's where the magic happens. And your fans won't forget it.

GET FANATICAL ABOUT FANS

"We're not competitor obsessed; we're customer obsessed. We start with the customer's needs, and we work backward."

—JEFF BEZOS

The Savannah Bananas should not exist today.

You can't name any of our players. We sell only one type of ticket. Our ballpark is almost a hundred years old. We don't have a digital scoreboard or any deluxe suites. We have zero corporate sponsors. We are run by a staff who mostly started as interns.

Everything we do is unconventional. None of it should work.

And yet ESPN has called the Bananas "the greatest show in baseball." *Sports Illustrated* has said our ballpark atmosphere "would make most MLB teams jealous." From that first sellout on opening night, we sold out seventeen additional games in our inaugural season—and every game since. Our waitlist for tickets is in the thousands. Fans travel from all over the world to see our show, sometimes paying scalpers up to ten times the ticket price just to get inside of Grayson's gates. Our social media following numbers are in the millions, surpassing those of many MLB teams. Hey, we've even won the Coastal Plain Championship a few times.

Not bad for a little team that everyone said would fail.

But how did we do it? How did we survive the long months of antagonism and indifference to make it to opening night? How did we survive an opening night where everything went wrong—where even the weather seemed dead set on seeing us fail?

Logan Moody said it best: Fans First.

And to keep fans first through all the challenges, you have to get a little fanatical.

YOU WOULDN'T BELIEVE...

"I didn't expect this, I don't think anybody expected this."

—TOM HASSETT, BANANAS FAN

Have you ever been a fan of something?

Have you ever felt so connected to a team, to a band, to a movie franchise, or to a brand that you want to reorient your whole life around it? Have you ever thought that maybe, just maybe, you were becoming a fanatic?

Maybe you grew up a die-hard fan of your local sports team, cheering them on no matter how high the highs or how low the lows. "You wouldn't believe the way this rookie plays center field!" you told your friends. And eventually one or two of them decided to come to the stadium with you to see what all the hype was about.

Maybe you fell in love with a music group, traveling out to your favorite concert spot every summer to watch them play. "You wouldn't believe what it's like once the band gets going and the crowd connects. There's no other experience like it," you said. The following summer, you got a few extra people in your van as you drove out to that year's show.

Maybe you just really love the local mom-and-pop diner in your town that no one else seems to know about. "It doesn't look like much, but you wouldn't believe their biscuits and gravy," you say to anyone who'll listen. So every time you have visitors in town, you take them out to eat there as a way of letting them in on your little secret.

Are you seeing the common theme here?

Three words: "you wouldn't believe."

These are the most powerful words in creating an unforgettable experience. They speak to something so outrageous, so surprising, so beyond expectation that there's only one possible response: tell the story to others.

That's what going Fans First is all about.

At Bananaland, our goal is to create "you wouldn't believe" moments at the ballpark every night.

You wouldn't believe what the break-dancing first base coach did in the fourth inning.

You wouldn't believe that a player came into the stands and delivered roses to my daughter.

You wouldn't believe there's a guy with a beard shaped like a banana.

"You wouldn't believe" moments transcend the experience itself. They're the ultimate form of word-of-mouth marketing—which we've found is far and away the best way to build awareness around your brand.

Don't believe me? Here are some stats for you. According to an Ogilvy Cannes Study, 74 percent of people say word of mouth is a key influencer in making decisions, and according to Nielsen, 83 percent of people trust the recommendations of family and friends over advertising.[1] [2]

---

1   Patrick Coffee, "Ogilvy Cannes Study: Behold the Power of Word of Mouth," *Adweek*. June 19, 2014, https://www.adweek.com/performance-marketing/ogilvy-cannes-study-behold-the-power-of-word-of-mouth/.

2   "Digital Formats Are Among the Most Trusted Advertising Sources Despite Slow Growth," Nielsen, September 28, 2015, https://www.nielsen.com/us/en/insights/article/2015/digital-formats-are-among-the-most-trusted-advertising-sources-despite-slow-growth/.

That's why, instead of spending a single dollar on traditional marketing, we go all-in on the "you wouldn't believe" moments. The results? Sold-out shows. A waiting list in the thousands. A social media presence that rivals many MLB teams.

What's even better than these "you wouldn't believe" moments is what they create: a "you wouldn't believe" life. You wouldn't believe what I've been able to do since founding the Bananas. You wouldn't believe what I get to do every day as part of my job. I know *I* still don't believe it—every day is a wonder for me.

When you believe in what you are doing and have fun while doing it, amazing things can happen.

That's why I'm sharing some of those moments in this book. Not so I can brag but so you, too, can create "you wouldn't believe" moments in your business—and ultimately build a "you wouldn't believe" life for yourself.

STOP CHASING CUSTOMERS

"For more than twenty years, I've said that every company must push self-renewal and reinvention, constantly challenging the status quo. For Starbucks, doing so means we are once again thinking big and dreaming big, embarking on a road we have not taken before."

—HOWARD SCHULTZ

Right now, I'm going to make a guess.

You're reading this book because you have a big question that you can't describe. You're hungry to learn more and become the leader your business deserves, but there's a piece of the puzzle that's missing, and you're not sure what it is.

Maybe you feel stuck, like you're not making progress the way you should, but you don't know why. Maybe you feel drained, like the passion you used to have for your work is gone, and you have no idea how to get it back. Or maybe your employees are quitting to go work somewhere else, and your customers are leaving you for other brands.

If this is you, then the "you wouldn't believe" life probably sounds like an impossible pipe dream.

It's not. All it takes to get there is a simple mindset shift.

There's something very, very wrong with what most people consider "business as usual" these days. Most organizations I talk to are focused on themselves. They all want to know the same thing: "How can I grow? How can I sell more? How can I make more money?" It's the wrong conversation. Even worse, it's driving the people who matter most to your brand, the people you should be engaging with—your customers and your employees—away.

Here are some more statistics for you:

- The average American company will lose up to 30 percent of its customers each year due to a lack of customer loyalty.[3]

- 74 percent of millennials will switch to a different retailer if they receive poor customer service.[4]

- 79 percent of people who leave an organization say that lack of appreciation is the main reason they left. Only 12 percent leave because of pay.[5]

These are the problems facing every business in every industry. They're the same problems that were waiting for us when we came to Savannah. At the time, we were an unknown team playing at the lowest levels of a boring sport in a town that didn't want us. By all measures, the cards were stacked against us, but we saw an opportunity to create something great.

Blockbuster, Kodak, Toys "R" Us, and Sports Authority had millions of customers. But they failed to stay relevant and reinvent themselves on their customers' behalf. They stayed the

3 Elizaveta Pavlovskaya, "70 Powerful Customer Retention Statistics You Need to Know in 2021," Semrush Blog, April 16, 2021, https://www.semrush.com/blog/customer-retention-stats/.

4 "Low Prices Raise Customer Loyalty," BusinessWire, August 15, 2017, https://www.businesswire.com/news/home/20170815005733/en/Low-Prices-Raise-Customer-Loyalty.

5 Gary Chapman and Paul White, *The Five Languages of Appreciation in the Workplace* (Chicago: Moody Publishers: 2019).

same, lost customers to other businesses, and either became shadows of their former selves or died completely.

There are a lot of reasons for these failures. But ultimately, their fundamental problem was the same: instead of delighting their fans, they were chasing customers.

That's the wrong target. Customers are transactional. Customers come and go. Customers can be replaced.

Customers aren't enough, even millions of them. Employees aren't enough, even the best. They aren't enough because *they can leave you*. If you haven't earned their enthusiasm, their devotion, their *fanaticism*, they'll move on to something bigger, better, more exciting, and more relevant.

Our solution? Stop chasing customers, and start creating fans.

Create fans of everyone you touch—customers, employees, friends, family, you name it. Be fanatical about creating fans. Act as if your business's entire life depends on it because it does.

Fans are there for the long haul. Fans are for life. Fans will drive halfway across the country during a pandemic just to catch one of your shows. Fans will mold their beards into bananas, volunteer for a male cheerleading squad even though they can't dance, and grab players' butts just to get a rise out of the crowd (note: butt-grabbing not recommended for most businesses in most circumstances).

We've learned that nothing is more important in building your business than creating fans, which means creating a business that puts Fans First.

How do you do that? You create something that makes *you* not just a fan but a fanatic.

EMBRACE YOUR INNER FANATIC

"I don't dislike baseball as a whole. I don't get professional baseball. But whatever they do in Grayson Stadium has me hooked for life! The whole stadium erupts when they play. Win or lose, the crowd still celebrates after every game. You will never leave Grayson without a smile on your face!"

—JUDITH POUNDERS, BANANAS FAN

Creating fans is an ongoing process of constant reinvention. It takes a vigilant eye, a curious mind, and an unwavering commitment to engineering the best experience possible.

In other words, to truly go Fans First, you must become a fanatic yourself.

Don't worry. Fanaticism can be a good thing. Seriously. Just look at Merriam-Webster's definition:

Fanatic: A person who is extremely enthusiastic about and devoted to some interest or activity.

See? There's nothing inherently negative about that. Fanaticism really can be as simple as having an abundance of love, admiration, devotion, or enthusiasm toward something you appreciate or find interesting.

In fact, I would argue that fanaticism is what drives us to reach our full potential, to stay laser-focused on what matters to us most. So I say let your fanaticism spill into every aspect of your business. Be fanatical about caring for people—on the field, in the office, in the stands, wherever the mood takes you. Be fanatical about send-offs: when your team leaves for the holidays or vacations, or even when they move on to other opportunities. Be fanatical about the details: the way emails are worded, the color of your packaging, the style of your bathroom decor.

Disney is fanatical. They pipe in the sound of a girl receiving voice lessons in a dead-end corner of Main Street. They have a team of full-time cast members whose sole job is to keep the mosquitoes away from guests. They carefully space out trash cans every thirty feet because that's the distance it took Walt to eat a hot dog and throw his wrapper away. When you're a fanatic, no detail is too small.

I'm fanatical too. I've trained my brain to never stop thinking about ways to create a better fan experience. Some might say that's dangerous. I say if you really want to have ultimate success and make the biggest difference, you need that fanaticism. It works because you love it. It works because you love yourself and what you're doing. When you're a fan, you'll always put in the effort needed to rise to the challenge in front of you.

Even the Bananas are fanatical. We know we're not a typical baseball team, and we'll never be a typical baseball team. Why? Because baseball as it's currently played is long, slow, and boring. Our fans deserve something better, something faster, something more exciting and more fun. They deserve baseball not as it is but as it *could be*.

That's the kind of fanaticism that drives us to experiment. That drives us to outthink other teams when we can't outspend them. That drives us to move fast and test every little idea. That creates all those "you wouldn't believe" moments that then get shared around the world.

That's the kind of fanaticism that creates fans.

We will never stop having fun and entertaining our fans. We will never stop asking how to create the best fan experience. We believe that when you stand for something bigger, then every detail, every moment, every action can make a difference.

Right now, you have a chance to make a difference too—not only in your business but in your life.

CHANGE THE CONVERSATION, CHANGE THE GAME

"Taking on a challenge is a lot like riding a horse,
isn't it? If you are comfortable while you are doing
it, you are probably doing it wrong."

—TED LASSO

At the Bananas front office, we rarely talk about how to create more revenue, sales, or profit.

Instead, we talk about creating fans. We talk about impact, about creating joy, fun, and excitement. We ask lots of questions. How can we eliminate friction for our fans? How can we entertain them? How can we invent on their behalf? How can we show up constantly and serve our fans at every turn? How can we be bigger fanatics?

If we answer those questions correctly, then we create more fans. And when we create more fans, we create more growth.

This singular, fanatical focus has made all the difference in the world.

Since 2016, the Bananas have grown more than we could have ever imagined—and we haven't even come close to hitting our ceiling (if there even is a ceiling).

Walt Disney once said, "Money doesn't excite me. My ideas excite me." I couldn't agree more. We've learned that the more fun you have, the more money you make. Yes, we're a baseball team. Yes, we're in the entertainment business. Yes, we've got a big stage to play on. But you don't need any of that to align your fans with your brand.

No matter what business you're in, every touchpoint, every interaction is an opportunity to create a fan, to thrill and delight the people who walk through your doors and buy your products and services. Those touchpoints are there for you to find. All you have to do is change your focus and change the conversation.

As you read through the rest of this book, here's my challenge to you: leave any notion of money and growth at the door.

Instead, as another famous Disney character said, "Let it go." Challenge the way things have been done in the past. Have the courage to do things others won't do. Break the rules in your industry, and stand for something better.

Above all else, embrace your inner fan. Remember how it feels to orient your whole life around something. And then work to create that feeling in your own business. Become a fanatic about it.

Be patient in what you want for yourself, but be impatient in how much you give to others.

If you're ready to do that, then let's get started.

In the following chapters, you're going to learn all about the Fans First Way. This is the recipe for success we've used to create a one-of-a-kind experience and transform the game of baseball. In part 2, you're going to learn how to bring the Fans First magic to your own business and life through what we call the Five Es. Then, in part 3, you'll learn how to grow success beyond your business and create a Fans First Movement.

Before you keep reading, a warning: things are about to get crazy. I said it at the beginning, but I'll say it again: this isn't your normal business book, and I'm not your normal author. Yes, you're going to get important lessons and takeaways. Yes, you're going to get a ton of stories and examples. But I've got other surprises in store for you too.

Later in the book, you will find one simple mindset that will be the single biggest game-changer in your career. It will bring more joy and fulfillment to your life than anything else I can share. It took me years to figure it out, but once I did, everything became clear, and my success multiplied more than I could have ever imagined.

The first fan is yourself.

You can't create fans until you are a fan of what you do.

This isn't about being successful just in work but in life. If you are not interested in, passionate about, and devoted to what you do, if you aren't driven to share what you do and tell everyone around you how excited it makes you, then you are missing out on life. You are not spending your time doing what matters and where you can make the biggest difference. You are not a fanatic.

I'm not saying quit your job or give up your obligations. But if you are not a fan of what you do, you will never do it to your full potential. And the world is missing out on what you can bring.

So find your fun and become your biggest fan.

If you can do that one thing, it will unlock all the other lessons I'll share with you here in this book. Instead of thinking about all the things you have to do, you'll start seeing new opportunities in your business—all the things you *get to do*.

So without further ado, it's showtime. Grab yourself a frosty Savannah Banana Beer or a sweet Banana Cream Soda. Put on your favorite slippers. Find your favorite recliner, and get comfortable. It's time to peel back the banana on the Fans First Way.

Enjoy Some S'mores

At one point in the classic '90s movie *The Sandlot*, Ham Porter and the new kid Smalls get into a funny conversation:

"Hey, you want a s'more?" Ham says.

Smalls looks confused. "Some more of what?" he says.

"No, do you want a s'more?" Ham replies, a little exasperated.

"I haven't had anything yet, so how can I have some more of nothing?"

"You're killing me, Smalls. These are s'mores stuff, 'kay? Pay attention. First, you take the graham. You stick the chocolate on the graham. Then, you roast the mallow. When the mallow's flaming, you stick it on the chocolate. Then you cover it with the other end. Then, you scarf. Kind of messy but good. Try some."

We'd like to share some s'mores with you too. Sadly, you can't eat these s'mores because edible book technology hasn't been invented yet. But you're still getting more—more ideas, more content, more fan stories, more banana puns, more everything.

Look out for sidebars like this one throughout the rest of the book—little snackable opportunities to learn and grow.

Part 2

BREAK THE RULES

"When you follow the crowd, you'll never draw a crowd."

—MIKE VEECK

Right now, you have a choice to make.

Do you want to play the same game as everyone else?

Do you want to be another unremarkable business?

Or do you want to change the game?

I opened this book with something we say a lot here in Banana-land: "Whatever's normal, do the exact opposite." Except when we first started, we weren't living by this maxim. In fact, we were doing everything exactly by the book. We were as normal as you could get. We were doing normal marketing like everyone else. We were posting normal social media like everyone else. We were making normal sales calls like everyone else. We learned quickly that normal gets normal results. Actually, in our case, the results were much worse.

We realized that to stay in business, we needed to make "normal" a four-letter word.

It wasn't until we made the decision to be different that everything started to change.

We vowed to play a different game. A game we could excel at—be best at. In my first book, *Find Your Yellow Tux*, I shared how I believe that everyone has something that makes them stand out and be the best version of themselves. Once you find that, the key is to amplify it by ten. That's your differentiator. That's your unique ability.

When you lean on that, you can change the game.

Look at what the rules of your industry are, and do the opposite. Break the rules. That's how you create something remarkable.

And if you're not scared, maybe you're not trying something big enough.

THE FANS FIRST WAY

"The only way to build a masterpiece is to start with a blank canvas."

—JIM COLLINS

Walt Disney's vision for Disneyland began on a park bench.

The year was 1948. Walt was at Griffith Park in Los Angeles with his daughters, Diane and Sharon, watching them have the time of their lives on the merry-go-round.

Seeing their pure, unbridled joy, he began to wonder: why wasn't there a place where children and parents could have fun together like this on a grander scale—a place where age didn't matter, a place where fun and fantasy were the law of the land?

Walt decided there should be. Soon, plans were underway to create Disneyland, the Happiest Place on Earth.

There was just one problem: everyone hated the idea.

Walt's brother and business partner Roy fought him tooth and nail. The banks thought he was crazy. His wife thought he'd bitten off more than he could chew.

Even other amusement park owners tried to talk him out of it. They attacked the concept from every angle. Where were the thrill rides? What was the point of building a castle that didn't do anything? Why was there only one entrance and exit?

Walt heard their criticism, but he understood something his critics didn't: the power of the imagination. The entrance, the ornate landscaping, the castle, and all those other little details weren't frivolous expenses. They were part of the magic.

While his brother, his bankers, and his peers in the amusement park industry only saw flowcharts and dollar signs, expenses and bottlenecks, Walt saw an opportunity to create an experience like nothing else in the world.

And he was right.

Today, Disneyland—along with the eleven other Disney theme parks that have sprouted up—is a beloved institution, drawing repeat fans from around the world. It's grown a bit since its debut in 1955, but the signature magic that Walt fought for still remains.

My vision for what would eventually become Bananaland also began on a bench—a dugout bench.

I was twenty-three, coaching some of the best players in the country in the best game in the world with the best seat in the house. And I was bored out of my mind.

I wasn't the only one. Outside of a few scattered fans, the ballpark was all but empty. No one was having any fun. The players played. The umpires made the calls, and the fans watched silently. Meanwhile, I was counting down the minutes until I got to go home.

I stopped being a baseball fan that day.

The game I had loved my whole life had lost its excitement, and I couldn't understand why. Where was the rule that said baseball had to be long, slow, and boring?

Baseball could be whatever someone dreamed it could be. It could become something completely different—something unique, something special, something brand new. All it needed was a little push in the right direction.

That's when I found my vision.

It wasn't seeing it to believe it; it was believing it to see it. I dreamed of a place where players, coaches, staff, and fans could all have fun together.

A place where everyone was a fan and fans always came first.

A place where the score didn't matter.

A place where fun led the way.

A place where we could dance, sing, cheer, and laugh together, no matter our age, our race, or where we came from.

A place where everyone could be kids again.

A place where baseball truly was a game that everyone could be a part of.

A place where every day, the stadium was packed and everyone was cheering and having fun.

This vision—to bring the fan experience back to baseball by being Fans First in everything we do—guides every decision we make. It guided our early baseball success in other cities. It guided our decision to come to Savannah. It guided us as we worked to win over a skeptical city and lay the foundation for what today we call Bananaland.

Bananaland is not an escape. It's the way life should be. It's fun for all different ages, all different races, for everyone all together. Bananaland is a place run by fun, where no one takes themselves too seriously and no one worries about what other people think. We sing, dance, laugh, and cheer. We make base-ball fun and live in each moment of fun.

For us, being Fans First led us to wanting to be the most fun team in baseball. What can you be the most of? Or as author Jeff Henderson says, "What do you want to be known for?" When you know that answer, every decision becomes easier.

Of course, the decision part is easy. It's the execution part that gets tricky. When you go Fans First, expect resistance. We've learned that if you aren't getting criticized, then you're playing it too safe.

In fact, in our experience, the most Fans First decisions are met with the most criticism. Any time you challenge the ways things are usually done, some people aren't going to understand what you're doing or why you're doing it—at least not at first. But as Jeff Bezos says, "You have to be willing to be misunderstood."

When we introduced the all-inclusive ticket with the all-you-can-eat concessions, we were misunderstood at first. When we introduced Banana Ball in 2020, some people thought we were making a mockery out of the game. Even when we decided to make Grayson Stadium completely ad- and billboard-free, a small but vocal group of people were angry.

This is why we started this section with a discussion of vision. The Bananas do a lot of crazy things, but it all ties back to that vision. We know what we want and why we're doing it. That's why, when we announce something surprising—like an ad-free ballpark—we lead the discussion with that vision. Here is what we said the day we announced the move:

> Our team, the Savannah Bananas, has decided to go all-in on the fan experience and eliminate all corporate sponsors from the ballpark, including billboards, signage, program ads and sponsor announcements.
>
> Instead of ads, we are giving the stadium back to the fans and celebrating the history of the 1926 ballpark. Every team that played at Grayson will now be featured on the wall. We've also unveiled the first-ever Fan Wall, where fans will get the chance to sign the wall before and after games.

When you don't have a responsibility to your corporate sponsors and your only responsibility is your fans, you can completely reimagine what the fan experience looks like.

We don't believe in trying to capitalize on our fans; we believe in trying to serve our fans better.

I believe you should never sell something you don't believe in. I believe in going all-in on the fan experience. I don't believe in ballpark advertising and would never buy it, so why would we sell it?

We will never stop asking the question, what will make a better fan experience? We don't believe anyone comes to a game to be advertised to or promoted to. People want fun, and it's our job to provide it!

When viewed through our ultimate vision—Fans First, Entertain Always—this decision was a long time coming, the logical next step toward creating the ultimate fan experience. It also got us a lot of attention—including a story in *The Washington Post*. Most people got what we were trying to do right away, flooding our announcement on Facebook with supportive comments:

> *Thank you. Focus on the fans and the game. Honor the players and staff. The product is excellent and the financial support is present! Yay team!*

> *Wow, that is powerful! Amazing vision! Thank you all for what you have done for Savannah!*

> *Jesse and crew, you are just all-in for the win! I love this!"*

But not everyone was bought in. Some greeted the move with skepticism and cynicism:

> I get this, but it feels a little like a stick in the eye of the businesses that helped you create your presence here.

> I don't understand this decision at all. I don't know a single fan who would be turned off by local ads around a ballpark.

> As a baseball fan, I don't mind the ads on the outfield wall. I could do without "That K was brought to you by so-and-so." What irritates me is all the junk in between innings.

Like the amusement park owners who hated on Walt's vision for Disneyland, these critics only saw our decision as a foolish break from the status quo. Without ad revenue, they said, we'd be dead and buried within a year.

Others were looking for the catch. Were we going to raise prices elsewhere to make up for lost revenue? (No.) Were we going to start charging for food at the ballpark? (Again, no.) Were we going to start adding convenience fees to our tickets? (Heck no!)

There was no catch. And as long as we remember who we serve (the fans), there never will be. Our mission is to create an experience so good that our fans feel like they're taking advantage of us.

Why? Because we know the real secret to success: long-term fans beat short-term profit.

Also, long-term fans *create* long-term profit.

In the year after we made our decision to go ad-free, our merchandise sales increased by over 200 percent—more than making up for any lost ad revenue.

And yet, so far, no one has copied us. We've proven you don't need ads to thrive, but they're happy to keep up with business as usual.

This isn't to say we won't partner with other sponsors and local businesses—we just won't do it with ads because ads don't add anything to the fan experience. If a partner or sponsor has a great idea for a promotion that *does* add to the fan experience, however, then we're 110 percent onboard.

If a company wants to do a promotion and give away a thousand free donuts to the crowd, then we'll go wild with that (especially if the donuts are banana-cream-flavored).

If another company wants to help us break the record for most people in banana costumes at a single event, then let's suit up.

But if Dole wants to partner with us to rename Grayson Stadium "Bananaland, presented by Dole," then forget it. (Nothing personal, Dole. If you're reading this, we'd still love to partner with you on the banana costumes idea.)

Ads detract from the fan experience, and we don't play that game anymore. We play our own game. And to do it, we had to break a few rules along the way.

We don't follow the long, slow, and boring rules of baseball. We don't follow the short-sighted rules of the business-as-usual crowd. We follow the Fans First Way—and we do it with our Five Es:

1. Eliminate friction

2. Entertain always

3. Experiment constantly

4. Engage deeply

5. Empower action

The Five Es have led in some crazy directions. We even developed a new game called Banana Ball, where batters can steal first base and fans can catch a foul ball for an out. As crazy as this sounds, it's all for our fans, and we will never stop asking how we can make the most Fans First experience in the world.

Every innovation, every new idea, everything we do starts and ends with the fans. First, we ask, "Is it Fans First?" Then, after we do it, we ask again, "Was that Fans First?"

That's what part 2 is all about. Get ready for some in-game action, a whole bunch of banana puns, and more surprises.

The Bananas Bookshelf

At the Bananas, we promote an active reading culture among our team. We even do book reports and everything. We believe that the more you're learning, the better you get at asking questions and the better you can serve your fans. At the end of every chapter, we're going to share some of the books that have informed our approach along the way. Here are a few suggestions to kick things off:

First Break All the Rules: What the World's Greatest Managers Do Differently by Marcus Buckingham

If It Ain't Broke, Break It: And Other Unconventional Wisdom for a Changing Business World by Robert J. Kriegel and Louis Palter

1st Inning

ELIMINATE FRICTION

*"Friction is anything that gets in the way of what
we want to accomplish in life, things that get in
the way of our hopes, our dreams, our aspirations,
and even our mundane day-to-day goals. It's the
big things that prevent us from being who we want
to be and those little things of doing what we want
to do. When brands fight friction, they don't just
create customers; they create evangelists."*

—JEFF ROSENBLUM

At a previous ballclub I worked for, we used to run a popular
promotion with Chick-fil-A. It was a stupid-cheap deal: for
$29.95, a family could get four tickets, four Chick-fil-A meals,
and four team hats.

The deal had some fine print. You could enjoy your Chick-fil-A,
and you could enjoy the ballgame, but you couldn't enjoy them
together. Why? Because, like most ballparks, we didn't allow
any outside food or drink in the stadium. We wanted to sell our
own concessions, so we did things the normal way.

The normal way isn't always right—especially if it's creating friction for your fans.

I remember one day, I was at the front gates welcoming guests when a happy family walked up to the ballpark with their Chick-fil-A order in hand, ready to enjoy their dinner with us at the game. I smiled and welcomed them, and then I pointed to the sign with all our rules. "I'm sorry, folks, but you have to eat up before you come through."

The family looked around for somewhere to sit. There weren't any benches, barricades, raised garden beds, errant folding chairs, or lush green lawn. Nothing.

With no other choice, they sat right on the hot summer pavement where they'd been standing. As they slowly ate their chicken in silence, I ate crow.

After they finished, they looked at me, then at the gates, then at each other. Then, without a word, they stood up, walked back to their car, and left.

Just like that, we lost a whole family of fans. All because of a nonsense policy that put profits over people (or even common sense).

But there's no rule that says an obstacle can't also be an opportunity. There's no rule that says disappointment is permanent. To make your business stand out, look at your industry's greatest perceived weaknesses, and make them your strengths.

I eliminated that policy the very next day. Then I vowed to eliminate friction from our shows wherever I saw it. You can't create an unforgettable experience if you can't empathize with your fans. You can't be loved until you stop doing what your fans hate.

Eliminating friction is about putting yourself in your fans' shoes and looking at every possible pain point, every possible frustration, every possible policy that slows things down, heats up tempers, and punishes fans.

Most companies think that company values and the policies they generate are about *them* and not the people paying for tickets. They don't always think about what the end goal should be: keeping their fans happy. Everyone thought I was crazy to eliminate our food and drink policy, that we'd lose a ton of money on concessions, and that we'd slowly crumble under the financial pressure.

We didn't. Instead, we made more fans—and those fans spent more money.

It's easy to think about the money you might lose in a decision like this. But think about the money you're losing by consciously allowing friction to dictate the fan experience. You'll lose more money in the long run by keeping friction in place than you will by making the Fans First choice.

Many of the best companies already understand this and actively look for ways to bring their fans' voices into the decision-making process:

- Starbucks leaves an empty chair at their meetings to represent their customers. For every decision they discuss, they ask how they can serve the person sitting in that chair.

- Chick-fil-A has two separate conversations when it comes to their most important decisions. The first conversation centers around adding more value for their customers, and the second is about creating more fans. They don't move forward with a decision until those two conversations are aligned.

- Disney filters every decision through its guest-first values. Disney's mission is to entertain, inform, and inspire people around the globe through the power of unparalleled storytelling. Their vision is to create magical moments for guests of all ages. Clearly, Disney likes to make money just like anyone else, but they know that they'll get the biggest revenue bump when their mission, vision, and values are connected.

You can eliminate friction in your business too—and in this chapter, you're going to learn how. As you move through these examples, remember: eliminating friction isn't passive. It should be part of your day-to-day processes.

Don't wait until you've forced a family to sweat through their Chick-fil-A meal on the hot pavement before fixing a policy or practice that's wrong. Get active and involved, and make sure it never comes to that in the first place. With every decision you make, with every practice you reevaluate, ask yourself:

- What does it look like when customers interact with your business's rules, policies, and spaces?

- Does a fan want this?

- Does this add value to a fan?

- Does this make life easier for a fan?

From there, let your values resonate outward in service of your fans. This might feel like a lot to think about at first, but we've found that it makes decision-making easier. Once you're looking for friction points, it's not hard to spot them—and to make a larger, lasting impact on the fan experience.

Take the Police Out of Policies

Why follow a policy, no matter how old or standard, that punishes your fans? Policies police your fans. And you don't want your policing to feel abusive. Question each policy. What's its purpose? Is it for the fans' benefit or yours? Are you benefiting in the way you want from this policy? Or do you just think you are? If fans can't see how a policy benefits them, it creates friction.

START WITH MACROFRICTIONS

"Too many rules get in the way of leadership. They just put you in a box. People set rules to keep from making decisions."

—COACH K

When it comes to the friction fans experience, there are two types: macrofrictions and microfrictions. Either can take very little time to fix or a lot of time to fix, depending on your creativity, your willingness to act, and other deciding factors.

Macrofrictions are the big friction points that are easier to spot. For instance, it wasn't hard to see that fans were getting burned by our Chick-fil-A promotion—in that one family's case, quite literally.

The biggest macrofriction the Bananas face is the sport they play. Baseball as traditionally played is long, slow, and boring.

There's no single solution to solving a macrofriction of that magnitude. But there are tons and tons of small ways to chip away at it. We've built our entire show around solving this macrofriction, working tirelessly to make sure our fans are always engaged and always have something to do. (We've even invented a whole new way to play the game that we call Banana Ball, but we'll get into that later.)

The second big macrofriction for us is the ballpark experience. Traditional sports teams have found a thousand and one ways to nickel-and-dime fans when they come to the ballpark, just like my former team and I did with our Chick-fil-A promotion. The Bananas believe that every pay point is a pain point. This is why we not only allow outside food and drink, but we also include all-you-can-eat concessions as part of our ticket.

This isn't a giveaway. Our tickets cost more than other independent-league teams. We're happy to charge a little more because we add more value. Most fans simply don't have the appetite to take advantage of our all-you-can-eat concessions, and we've found Bananas fans spend twice as much while at the ballpark as fans at other stadiums do.

Another industry that's notorious for nickel-and-diming their fans is the airline industry, especially economy airlines. They'll advertise a cheap ticket to make you feel like you found a sweet deal. But once you've clicked through on that sweet deal, they bury you in charges. A charge to pick a seat. A charge to check your bags. A "convenience" charge for buying the tickets that feels anything but. A charge to order food.

Then, just to add insult to injury, once you're on the flight, they'll try to sell you a credit card while you're sitting in the seat you paid for.

No one enjoys being dragged kicking and screaming through the typical ticketing process. It's no wonder, then, that when given a choice, people will gladly choose an airline that doesn't actively make them miserable.

Enter Southwest Airlines.[6] During the Great Recession of 2008 through 2010, the airline industry was struggling. Most carriers responded by finding new ways to nickel-and-dime their travelers. Southwest's own teams of consultants and financiers said the airline could add $350 million in revenue if they charged for bags like everyone else was doing. But the execs gave that idea a hard pass. They wanted to "democratize the skies" and felt extra baggage fees would "make it harder for people to fly, not easier."

Instead, they doubled down and, with Roy Spence's "Bags Fly Free" campaign, made a big deal of being one of the only airlines with no checking fees. It took less than a year for Southwest to add more than $1 billion to their bottom line, gain market share, and give big bonuses to their employees all because the execs stuck to their values by not adding friction to their customers' experience.

Think long-term values over short-term profits. Make fans' lives easier, not harder.

People don't want add-ons. They want the real price upfront because it makes them feel respected. Fans will pay more for an all-inclusive ticket when they know the value they're getting, just like they'll pay more for a flight if it means they won't get shaken down for more money every step of the way. If you're not sure what your macrofrictions are in your business, just ask your fans. They know all too well, and they'll be happy to share with you.

---

6 Mark Schenk relates this story in a 2018 podcast by Anecdote International. The full version of this story is in Lisa McLeod's *Selling with Noble Purpose: How to Drive Revenue and Do Work That Makes You Proud.*

No Fees, Please

Every pay point is a pain point. Every time a fan has to pay, it creates friction. Examine your fans' buying experience, ease of transactions, and line items on receipts. Make these as simple as possible. And for Split's sake, get rid of those fees!

ZOOM IN ON MICROFRICTIONS

"It's just not that difficult to be kind. It's not that difficult to use positive language, like 'my pleasure' instead of 'no problem,' which is two negative words back to back."

—MARIE MATZINGER, FANS FIRST DIRECTOR

Microfrictions are the little details that chafe and scratch at fans, even if the fans don't realize it. They can be a lot harder to spot, but they can make a massive difference in how your fans interact with your business. Once you learn how to spot them, you'll be like the kid in *The Sixth Sense*. Everywhere you look, you'll see a thousand small, avoidable annoyances.

Microfrictions cover a broad range of practical everyday things—invoices, emails, voicemails, and the like. You can test for them anywhere.

For instance, go to your website and see how easy it is to

navigate. What happens when you click a link? How easy is it to find the information you want? To buy a product? To find your phone number? Once they find your phone number, what's the fan experience of calling you?

Banks and financial institutions are the worst at this. You have to go through so many menus, enter so many personal numbers, get disconnected, and then go through it all again before you finally get a person on the line who can help you figure out why your debit card didn't work.

The death of video rental stores had a lot to do with microfrictions too. The constant rewind reminders, late fees, short rental periods, and physical pickups and drop-offs. And then the new movie you wanted might not be there.

We audit every fan touchpoint constantly, and we're always discovering and correcting new microfrictions. For instance, the phone number on our website wasn't always so prominent. Now it's huge. Seriously, you can't miss it.

Once we identified that microfriction, we audited the whole phone experience to not only eliminate other microfrictions but also to create an unforgettable experience. Our voicemail is currently a parody of Camila Cabello's "Havana": "Savannah nah nah, you've reached the Savannah Bananas nah, nah, nah."

Our hold music is equally entertaining: "Ring, ring, ring, ring,

ring, ring, Banana Phone." Every couple of weeks people call us and ask to be put on hold. It makes zero sense, and it makes complete sense. People want something different and will always seek that out. I think it's crazy—hanging out on hold is not my idea of a good time—but that's why we love our Bananas fans.

Can you imagine calling a business just to hear their hold music? Have you ever done it? If you have, then stick with that business. They know what it means to be Fans First.

Unfortunately, that's not what most businesses do. Instead, they'll put you through a maze of menus to answer even a simple question. If you're lucky, at the end of that maze, you'll get to talk to an actual living, breathing human being. More likely, you'll get pushed to voicemail—and then no one will ever follow up with you. I once called ten landscaping companies for quotes, and only three called me back. Talk about a perfect storm of microfrictions—not to mention a terrible way to create fans.

That's why we do things differently. As Marketing Director Kara Heater says, "When we respond, we want people to know that there is a real human being behind every comment, every interaction."

See? It's simple. Just by being there, you can take a lot of pain out of someone's day and make them feel cared about.

Drop the Surveys

Henry Ford once said, "If I had asked people what they wanted, they would have said faster horses." We don't ask our fans what they want. But we're always watching and listening to see what they might tell us.

Every game, we observe our fans closely. We even take pictures of our grandstands at different points in the game so we can learn how and when our fans sit down and get up, how full our stadium is at different parts of the game, and when our fans leave. Asking fans if they think our games should be shorter would not get real results, but watching to see how they respond to the show does. This is another way we put ourselves in our fans' shoes to make sure we're always being Fans First.

AUDITING FAN FRICTION

"Sometimes you need to immerse yourself with the fans and walk their path to know what they're feeling."

—EMILY COLE,
CO-OWNER OF THE SAVANNAH BANANAS

Sometimes friction finds you. More often, you have to find the friction.

The Bananas don't just find friction. We fight it.

Every team member is always on the lookout for pinch points, from the lines at the concessions stand to the trash on the ground. This isn't by accident. We look for friction fighters when we're interviewing new team members by staging trash on the concourse. If the candidate stops to pick it up as we're walking through the ballpark, then we've learned something very important about their character.

Picking up trash is an easy thing to do—the Fans First thing to do. But a small act speaks volumes. If they're willing to overlook those little bits of trash, what else are they willing to overlook?

By focusing on creating friction fighters from the get-go, we're able to set a high baseline for our fan experience. But we don't stop there. To ensure a friction-free fan experience, we're constantly designing and conducting what we call friction audits. Here are a few ways we go about it.

The Undercover Fan

"You can observe a lot just by watching."

—YOGI BERRA

For years, Walt Disney lived part time in a Main Street apartment at Disneyland. It was the perfect home base for him to conduct some undercover ops. Whether fans realized it or not,

Walt was always walking the park, often in disguise, to better understand the Disneyland guest experience. He told his animators and cast members to do the same.

In our third season, we realized that the Bananas once again had an opportunity to learn from Walt. We'd done well the past couple of years, but we knew we had some weak spots. Some of them we knew; some of them we didn't. To uncover those unknowns, we decided to put ourselves in our fans' shoes. How long did it take to park, to stand in line, to get food, to find a seat? We realized we didn't know—and what you don't know, you don't control.

Thus was born the "Undercover Fan" program. Every game night, someone on our team would disguise themselves and attend as a regular fan. Throughout the game, they would take notes on their experience, focusing on friction points. Then, they'd share their experience with the team at the end of the game. What frustrated them? What bored them? What experience was less than stellar?

Every member of the team is an Undercover Fan eventually— our freshest interns, our seasonal team members, our full-time employees, and even our president Jared. We love the variety of perspectives this gives us. Someone from operations is going to see different pinch points than someone in entertainment. But no matter who's out there in the stands, not a single game goes by where we don't learn something important and adjust accordingly.

The first night I got to play Undercover Fan (wearing my ingenious disguise of *not* a banana-yellow tuxedo), things bottomed out quickly—or at least my car did as I drove into a giant pothole immediately after pulling into the parking lot. Then, as I got out of the car, I saw that our parking penguins (yes, even our parking lot attendants are part of the show) had their backs toward me and were eating burgers. Not cool, penguins.

As the game progressed, I saw other friction points that surprised me. I also made sure to talk to the fans and get their perspective. The best part? No one recognized me. "Normally there's a crazy guy in a yellow tuxedo running around," one fan said. "He usually runs the show. He's bizarre. He's an owner, and he throws stuff into the crowd. Not sure where he is tonight, though."

If he only knew.

I don't strike up these conversations to stroke my ego. Being an Undercover Fan is serious business. As an owner, I revel in these moments. They're some of the best ways for me to get direct, unfiltered feedback from our fans. Sometimes, a fan will give me a rundown of the show and talk about all the things they enjoy. Other times, a fan will surface a big problem that none of us were aware of.

That's the huge gift of the Undercover Fan program. As an owner or a president of a company, you may see the ideal of how things are, but this is not the reality that fans experience. As my wife Emily puts it, "Things that are obvious to an employee aren't necessarily obvious to a fan or customer. Something as simple as finding the entrance to an office can be tricky for someone who has yet to do it. We as employees walk in those doors multiple times a day and forget that someone showing up at a large facility for the first time might need extra signage showing them where to park and enter."

We've made tons of changes because of our Undercover Fan observations. We added shade to sunny areas and lights to the dark parking lot. We changed the length of the game and the sound level of the speakers. We made changes to how we form lines, to where our parking penguins are stationed, to how we prepare our food. We even changed the wording on our tickets because people thought GA stood for "Georgia" instead of "general admission." I wouldn't have thought of that one in a million years.

Oh, and we fixed those potholes too.

Sometimes a fan has a bad experience and doesn't say anything—or at least they don't say anything to us. Like the family forced to eat their Chick-fil-A out on the sidewalk, they just leave and never come back.

This is why the Undercover Fan program is so important. If you're waiting for your fans to come and tell you about every problem, then you're going to be waiting for a long time. Better to get out there and find the problems for yourself.

On the Front Line

"When the nacho cheese runs out, everything slows down."

—"TOBY"

The next step up from the Undercover Fan is the frontline worker. Where the Undercover Fan allows you to walk around and experience the show as a fan, the frontline worker gives you the experience of actually serving the fans on the front lines.

Just like with the Undercover Fan, we all take our turns as frontline workers. When it was my turn, I once again ditched my yellow tux, got a staff shirt, and put on my name tag. For that night, I was Toby—and Toby was ready to grill the heck out of some burgers.

Or so I thought. Did you know that grilling hundreds of burgers in sweltering heat for two hours is really, really hard work? The grease and sweat soak into your clothes and your hair. The pace is relentless, and the work is monotonous. (Also, the smell of all that grease will follow you around for days afterward, like the ghost of burgers past.)

I was exhausted by the end of that run. More importantly, I understood how exhausted our regular team members must feel by the end of every shift. I now had a new respect for what they had to endure every day as part of a regular shift.

Of course, my shift was just beginning. After cooking came cashiering—and no one felt like taking it easy on old Toby. They put me on the busiest register in the stadium right at five thirty. Before we'd even opened, a line was already forming in front of me.

So did Toby make it through okay? He did not. He was a disaster. He couldn't run the register properly. He couldn't remember the menu. He couldn't even get burgers to fans without dropping them.

Don't feel sorry for Toby, though. He figured it out...eventually.

About forty minutes in, I finally got a feel for what I was doing and started making the experience fun. I went over the top. If someone ordered cookies, I would juggle a few packages and ask the fan to point to the one they wanted.

Soon, the rest of the team joined in on the antics. We weren't just serving Cokes. According to Patrick, we were serving "the best Coke of your life." The more we got into it, the more the fans got into it—and the more our service improved.

I guess the math isn't hard. Better service + a better show = better wait times and happier fans. And for a little bonus math, it also resulted in a brimming-full tip jar (Toby gave his share to the rest of the team).

We learned some big lessons that day. First, we realized that we had been so wrapped up in just serving, in completing every transaction at warp speed, that we forgot that concessions were part of the show too. By leaning into the show, we also reduced a big friction point.

Second, I learned the importance of being empathetic with your staff, of putting yourself in their shoes and doing what they do so they know that *you* know what their experience feels like. This camaraderie allows you, as the boss, to effectively up the energy for everyone around you (what psychologists would call "affect contagion"). Without this kind of commitment, work becomes just that: work. And where's the fun in that?

The frontline worker experience was so eye-opening that Jared even set up a new front-office position: Director of First Impressions. No single person occupies this role—it rotates from person to person year round. Everyone works different shifts, with serving the fans as their only job.

FAQS: THEY ASK, YOU ANSWER

"I want you to know I value each of your opinions, even when you're wrong."

—TED LASSO

A few years ago, I invited Marcus Sheridan, author of *They Ask, You Answer* and self-proclaimed struggling pool guy, to join me on my podcast, *Business Done Differently.* During our discussion, Marcus shared how he started the swimming pool company River Pools and Spas with two buddies in 2001. Things were going okay up until the economy crashed in 2008. Within forty-eight hours of the crash, he had lost $250,000 in business. Over the coming weeks, it got worse. By January 2009, the company was looking at bankruptcy, which would have lost Marcus and his partners their homes and sixteen employees their jobs. They had to pull back from the edge without spending any money.

He realized customer engagement was the key. If he obsessed over addressing their questions—the good, bad, and ugly— through text, video, and website, he might save the business.

Soon, he was answering every pool-related question imaginable on his website. Whatever a customer asked, he wrote a blog or recorded a video and then shared it publicly. His pool company soon became the resident experts on fiberglass pools—and the go-to for anyone looking for those pools. Now they've become the largest manufacturer and installer of fiberglass pools in the world.

Marcus's story taught us to monitor friction by taking a close look at what our fans are saying—specifically, what kinds of questions they're asking. Bananas co-owner Emily Cole spearheads this effort, reading every single message that the fans submit online. Serving on the friction-fighting frontlines, she has learned some valuable lessons:

1. **Get clear.** If you get the same question from multiple people, clearly answer this question by updating the language on your website and any other communication platforms you are using.

2. **Go deeper.** Listen to the fans' true interest and provide more details on that. For example, if someone wants to know about handicap parking locations, expand your answer to include the location of ramps in the ballpark, handicap seating options, and wait service for food and drink.

3. **Stay connected.** Reading every fan inquiry can feel like a lot, but it's a great way to stay connected with your team, to keep a pulse on what your fans care about, and to understand how you can serve them better.

Staying connected has taught all of us what it means to truly be there for a diverse fanbase made up of different races, ages, genders, backgrounds, abilities, and nationalities. By hearing the kinds of questions they ask, we learn how to better serve them.

When it comes down to it, all our friction-fighting efforts help us to stay focused on the metrics that matter most. Too many businesses only track and measure the metrics they think they're supposed to. We only track the things that will help us achieve our goals faster—specifically, to deliver an unforgettable Fans First experience.

As we've learned through all of our various friction audits, sometimes the issue that matters most isn't even on your radar. That's okay. That's *good*, even—as long as you have a program in place to unearth it and learn. Then, once you have, you can measure it, manage it, and make that friction go poof!

What Do You Hate about Your Customer Journey?

After I gave a keynote speech to a large car dealership in Ohio, the entire staff and their spouses got together and made a list of all the things they hated about the car-buying experience. After listing out a hundred-plus items, they realized they needed a new plan of attack.

Have you ever listed out all the things you hate about your own customer journey? Get together with your company's team, and list out all the things you hate about your industry's primary fan experience. Go to town—no idea is too small. Finally, create a plan of attack. Identify the biggest friction points, and have an Ideapalooza on how you'll work to address them.

EVERY GAME IS SOMEONE'S FIRST GAME

"All the MLB games were just that: games. The Bananas put on a show."

—ROBERT GARY, BANANAS FAN

Imagine you work at a hot dog stand. You can create the best hot dog stand in the world—with the best condiments, the softest buns, and the cleanest utensils. Every aspect of the experience can be carefully thought out, from the design of the stand to the ease of payment at the register.

At the end of the day, though, you're still selling hot dogs.

And there ain't much you can do to improve that.

That's the fundamental macrofriction we've faced with the Bananas. We can have the best show, the most entertaining promotions, the greatest fan experience around. But at the end of the day, we're still playing baseball—and baseball as traditionally played is long, slow, and boring.

The first several years of the Bananas have been focused on solving every friction we could control around the game. The future of the Bananas is to create a better hot dog—that is to play a better, more exciting version of baseball.

Ultimately, that's what eliminating friction is all about.

True failure, the permanent kind, comes when businesses keep doing things the way they've always been done. Or worse, it comes from doing nothing.

Eliminating friction is doing the opposite. It's about finding solutions. It's about taking action. It's about committing to being better.

Often this isn't easy. Friction fighting will likely feel pretty tough at first, especially when you come up against a problem that can't be solved overnight.

For most people, that's when the resistance sets in. Why put in the time and energy to change what you're doing if you're already making good money anyway?

Because friction fighting isn't about winning in the short term. It's about investing in the long term.

Remember that family that had to eat Chick-fil-A on the scorching sidewalk? If I was only thinking short term, then I wouldn't have seen the problem. We got their $29.95. Who cares if they didn't go to the game?

You can see the problem with this kind of thinking. Long term, how much money did we miss out on by losing them as fans? How many other future fans did we lose as a result?

Dump "old" and "reliable." That doesn't get butts in seats. That doesn't earn you fans.

Instead, treat every day as if someone is about to interact with your brand for the first time. How do you make that experience new? How do you make it *remarkable*?

The Bananas Bookshelf

Friction: Passion Brands in the Age of Disruption by Jeff Rosenblum

They Ask, You Answer: A Revolutionary Approach to Inbound Sales, Content Marketing, and Today's Digital Consumer by Marcus Sheridan

2nd Inning

ENTERTAIN ALWAYS

> *"I would rather entertain people and hope they learned something than educate people and hope they were entertained."*

—WALT DISNEY

"**R**eady to get hit in the balls?"

This isn't the usual text a boss sends to one of his team members, but it is the text I sent to Patrick Briody one day as he was headed back to Grayson Stadium from lunch.

The message had zero context, but at this point, Patrick didn't need any. Part of the OG 2016 intern squad, Patrick has been with the team since the beginning, putting both his pride and his body on the line in the name of showing our fans a good time.

Patrick has just about done it all for the cause of fun. He's donned the Split suit more times than he can count. He's starred in tons of Bananas videos, playing a bodyguard for pigs, reenacting Tom Cruise's famous underwear scene from *Risky*

Business, and now, taking a banana in the nanners to tease the upcoming season. It was an outrageous idea for a promotion, and Patrick was usually up for anything we threw at him. But to tell the truth, I really wanted to see his reaction to this...throw.

For the record, I would never force Patrick or anyone else to do a stunt they were truly uncomfortable with. The text was more an offer than a command. But Patrick was game to take one (okay, several) for the team. So once he arrived back at the ballpark, we headed back down to the field, and Patrick got ready for some pain.

In our idea for our latest video, Patrick would be on the phone when suddenly he got pelted in his nether region. But when it came time to shoot the scene, Patrick was understandably protective of his bits. Every time I lobbed a banana his way, he reflexively blocked in and pretended he got hit.

I couldn't blame him. But I also couldn't let that slide. "Sorry, bud," I said. "It really needs to hit you."

"You've lost your mind!" Patrick said as he chuckled and got back into position. Then, he took a deep breath and took a 'nana to his nanners.

And now Patrick is a star. People still bring up that video and tell him how much it made their family laugh. "Those moments are what it's for," Patrick says. "Never take yourself too seriously. You might just bring joy to people's lives."

I couldn't agree more. That's why one of the Bananas' Five Es is to entertain always.

Every business is in the entertainment business. It doesn't matter if you build houses or run a hotel. If you are not entertaining your customers, you won't have customers to entertain. The definition of entertain is to provide enjoyment and amusement, and these provisions are essential for building future fans. And really, don't we all want to provide enjoyment to our customers?

As PT Barnum said, "The noblest art is making someone happy."

People are hungry for things that bring them joy and fun. Even in serious industries, there's still an opportunity to make the fan experience easier and more enjoyable. Take a divorce attorney (yes, I've given myself a challenge with one of the most unfun jobs I can think of). How are legal papers delivered? How are emails worded? Does the decor in the waiting room give your clients confidence and reassurance? Can they easily find help to translate jargon? What about a humanizing pair of fun socks? A break-up playlist to lighten some tension?

As a business, you're hosting people. That's why Disney calls customers guests. As a host, it's your job to entertain. To make things easy. To make guests feel comfortable and valued, no matter the situation. That's why at Disneyland, when a child is too small to go on a ride, the cast member presents the child with a Future Rider card. It invites the child to come to the front of the line once they reach the height requirement. Just like that, disappointment is turned into promise, which is then turned into a whole lot of fun.

That's what lobbing bananas at Patrick's nanners was all about—upping the ante, raising expectations, giving people a good time, and *entertaining always.*

Of course, a shot in the nanners is, well, low-hanging fruit. Clearly, we're not above the cheap laughs, but we've got a whole arsenal of tricks up our sleeve. After all, in Bananaland, baseball is not a spectator sport. From the moment the gates open to when the last fan leaves, we jam our feet down on the entertainment pedal, and we never let up. In this chapter, you're going to learn how to do the same.

THE SEVEN STAGES OF ENTERTAINMENT: FIRST TO LAST IMPRESSION

"All the world's a stage,

And all the men and women merely players."

—WILLIAM SHAKESPEARE

Here's the first thing to understand about entertaining always: always means always. All the world's a stage, and you can make any experience fun.

If we did things the normal way, we'd look at Grayson Stadium and say that we had one stage: the field. When the announcer yells, "Play ball," we can start our show.

Spoiler alert: we don't see it that way. Yes, the baseball game happens on the field, and yes, we entertain there, but most of our show happens off the field. From the very first moment a fan or future fan interacts with us, we are entertaining on one of the following seven stages.

Stage One: The First Impression

Everything the Bananas do is about bringing fans to Bananaland and showing them a really, really good time. If we can entertain the fans on their home turf, it encourages them to come to ours.

That's why our first stage isn't at Grayson Stadium at all. It's our website, our social media channels, even our tickets.

Can you *really* turn your tickets into a stage? Split yeah, you can. When a fan buys a ticket, they get a payment confirmation celebration video, a thank-you call, and even a pregame music playlist for the drive to the ballpark.

That last bit was former Ticket Experience Coordinator (and now Finance Director) Matt Powell's idea. "I always thought that we did a great job entertaining our fans during our games, but I really put myself in our fans' shoes and realized that the journey begins before the game even starts," Matt says. So he set out to curate an epic, uplifting pregame playlist, getting recommendations from Head Coach Tyler Gillum and a slew of players and front office folks. Now we have a new way to get fans hyped before they even get to the park!

Why do we put so much into entertaining even when our fans are at home? It's right in our values: Fans First, Entertain Always. When people come to our website, when they check us out on social media, or when they groove to our playlist on the way to a game, these are their first impressions of what we're all about, and we have to make it stick.

Stage Two: The Parking Lot

The first thing you see when you come to the parking lot is our friendly parking penguins. You met them in the last chapter, even if they were eating burgers at the time. As you get out of your car and move through the lot, our mascot Split will also be there to greet you and pose for some pictures. Then, you'll meet our greeters, decked out in some appealing banana costumes and ready to check your tickets and answer any questions. Just a flash of peel, to whet the appetite.

Stage Three: The Plaza

You've seen this script already. It's the pregame march that we opened the book with. Nothing like kicking off the show with a little song and dance!

But here are a few more examples from our everyday repertoire.

There's always a DJ in the plaza playing throughout the entire game. Princess Potassia graces the scene in her trademark bright-yellow dress, singing well-known Disney songs gone Bananas and stopping to take pictures with little kids. Coming out of COVID-19 shutdowns, she made good on the Disney moment, sitting on the outfield wall as the sun was setting while parodying *Frozen*'s "For the First Time in Forever," with all the lyrics rewritten to acknowledge how long we'd all been waiting for a Bananas game.

Stage Four: The Concourse

Every touchpoint means every touchpoint. Always means always. (Are you starting to get the theme here?)

The concourse is full of fun touchpoints. We have a pep band marching around, singalongs with characters, jugglers, unicyclists, magicians—it's a regular circus. But let's zoom in to one place you would never expect to be entertained: the bathroom.

The evolution of our bathroom started with our Macon Bacon urinal cakes. The Macon Bacon is our first rival, after all, and we couldn't pass up the chance to let fans douse them. These days, there are all kinds of touches, from "Taking Care of Business" piping in over the speakers to surprise solos from one of our sax or tuba players in the stall next door—which, of course, will either make your day or scare the crap out of you. Either way, mission accomplished.

Me, I'm a sucker for our "no farting" signs. The only problem with those is that people keep stealing them. But that's a friction for us, not the fans. At least we know they love 'em.

As I write this, a few of Grayson's bathrooms have just undergone a big renovation. The bathrooms are all-out banana-themed. Gold toilets and gold toilet paper bedeck the "nicest stalls in the world." We even have a working banana phone—you know, just in case you need someone to talk to while you're doing your business. Finally, we've added plenty of mirrors: a "self-checkout" mirror, a "second self-checkout" mirror, and, of course, a carnival mirror for splits and giggles.

Never underestimate the power to make an impression—and to entertain—with normally neglected spaces.

Everything tells a story, and everywhere is a place to entertain.

Stage Five: The Grandstands

The game is about to kick off—and we're about to turn the show all the way to eleven.

We head into the crowd to the fans cheering, yelling, and screaming. All our characters get in on it. The break-dancing first base coach. The Banana Nanas. The Man-Nanas. The acrobats. The paraders throwing Mardi Gras beads. The players delivering roses. Even the players who aren't starting the game get into the act. Our goal: boost the crowd's energy one more time so we can kick off the show with a bang.

I'm in the crowd, too, throwing underwear around. Because who wouldn't want a pair of Dolce and Bananas chucked at them from a stranger? We're currently working on a T-shirt cannon—banana-shaped, of course—for added distance.

Every fan is a winner in Bananaland, but only the loudest fans get these hot, hot undies. I've found it's usually the newest fans who are most willing to get crazy. They're fresh to the ballpark. They see the madness all around them, and they realize that the only way to win is to go all-in.

I remember one guy in particular who went crazy, ripping his shirt off and howling like there was no tomorrow. I fired over those premium Fruit of the Loom...and he promptly proceeded to put them on over his clothes. And there they stayed all night. What a sight.

There's no better stage than the one you make for your fans. Not only is it a great way to break down the barriers between us and them, but it also serves as that final reminder that this is not your typical baseball game, and we are not your typical baseball team—and that anything can happen during the show.

Stage Six: The Ballfield

This is the obvious stage. And obviously, we play baseball here, but that's not all we do. There's always something going on down on the field—between pitches, between innings, during mound visits, and so on.

Our bat boy dresses as Batman and gets his own theme music when he runs out to retrieve the bats. During pitching changes, pitchers come out on Segways, banana boats, motorcycles, pedi-cabs, you name it. Players come up to bat with their own march-ing band, with their own red-carpet show, or with a caddie and a monogrammed golf bag.

Opposing players come in expecting shenanigans, but nothing can prepare them for the experience. The same goes for the umpires—which is why I always meet with them to mentally prepare them before a show. "There will be break-dancing first base coaches," I start. "Also, you might get a massage from some-one in a Barney costume, or a grandma may bring you cookies and tea in the middle of the game."

They usually look a little perplexed, but better to get them in on the joke so they don't feel like they *are* the joke.

Stage Seven: The Last Impression

"The last impression leaves a lasting impression."

—SHEP HYKEN

After the show wraps and the fans start heading out of the gates, we have a little surprise waiting for them as well. After all, we want a fan's last impression to be as good as their first impres-sion. How many businesses do you know that pay just as much attention to you as you're walking out as when you're walking in?

So what do we do for our last impression? I can't give away all our secrets—at least, not yet. You'll have to keep reading to find out.

SCRIPTING THE FAN EXPERIENCE

"Control your controllables. Control your own experience. Control the opening shot and the last shot."

—WALT DISNEY

To recap, the first step of entertain always is to entertain always. Every part of your business is a stage, from your website to your invoices, and it's up to you to put on a show.

But entertaining isn't all about randomly taking a banana in the nanners. Believe it or not, there is a method to our madness. We have learned to script out the entire fan experience at every touchpoint and every part of the show. No detail is too small. If we can think about it, then we can control it.

Here, we're taking a page from the best. At the Masters, golf's premier tournament (if you're counting, that's two golf references in this chapter—didn't expect that, did you?), they dye brown spots on the grass green. They pipe in the sound of birds chirping. They treat the water so it is crystal clear. They only sell their merch at Augusta National. They have very few commercials and very few sponsors.

The event is so carefully curated that it's the talk of the golf world every year. Their tickets are elusive—and exclusive—and therefore highly desirable. They don't have to worry about marketing. Their seamless experience sells it for them.

If you run a business, you can script your experience. It starts with identifying your stages and mapping your fan journey from the first touchpoint to the last. If you need to play Undercover Fan or frontline worker to better understand that journey, then so be it—whatever it takes to know what your fans experience at every step.

Here are the principles we follow to make sure our show never goes off the rails.

Let Fun Lead the Way

"People don't care how you feel. You need to paint pictures; you need to tell stories. That's what people want. They want to be entertained. Then all the other stuff kind of filters across as part of the whole thing."

—GLEN FREY

You need a plumber, and you have no idea who you need to call. So you do a quick Google search and find someone who looks interesting. When you call, you hear a toilet flush. When he shows up, he's dressed like Super Mario. When he encounters a tough clog, he breaks out his golden plunger. Then, when he's done, he leaves behind a rubber ducky on top of your toilet.

Are you going to call that guy again next time you need some plumbing work?

I'm guessing you will. How could you not?

When considering the fan experience you want to create, let fun lead the way. Ask yourself how you want to make your fans feel, and then look at every detail of your experience to make sure it aligns with that feeling.

Leave Room for the Magic

> *"We're living in a time where we want to be entertained, but I think part of what people are looking for, that they don't even know they're looking for, is to be uplifted in many ways."*
>
> —GIANCARLO ESPOSITO

Scripting the fan experience is a living, breathing exercise. Map it out, but don't write it in stone.

We iterate all of our scripts, adding something new to the experience each time. Every time, we ask, "Is that the *best* fan experience? Is that *still* creating fans? Have we just sunk into normalcy here?"

This is how we blend creativity and spontaneity with our scripted experiences.

Our teammates aren't robots. They're living humans making decisions in the moment to provide the best possible experience for every fan. Yes, there's a script to follow, but that script just paints the broad strokes. Everyone on the Bananas is free to add their own touches and strokes of genius.

Sometimes, the best moments are neither scripted nor ad-libbed. They're serendipitous. For instance, whenever the Macon Bacon comes to town, someone on our team dresses up in a pig costume with a sign that says, "Save the pigs. Stop making bacon." They'll wander all throughout Grayson stadium that way, all to the tune of Sarah McLaughlin's "Angel."

One night, we couldn't find the staffer who usually puts on the pig costume. So I found Brian, our Sexy Saxophonist (that's another story) and asked if he could jump into the costume. He did, but something was different. From the dugout, I could see fans taking tons of pictures and laughing a little more than usual.

As it turned out, Brian had put the costume on backward in his hurry to get it on. That little corkscrew tail hanging down in front looked like something else.

We wouldn't have scripted something like that, but it sure was entertaining.

Keep Fighting Friction

"I love our team, and I want them to go as far as they can every year. But the entertaining is a bit more important to me. If we start out 0–30, it would be a bummer for our organization, but I'm still going to be just as enthusiastic. I believe we could still have sellout crowds playing .300 ball."

—MARTY JONES, THE MAIN MAN-NANA

It was a normal day in the Bananas front office. I walked up to my wife Emily's desk with a big grin on my face.

"I shipped my underwear!"

Emily looked at me, confused, and said, "You what?"

"I shipped my underwear...for free!" I added, holding up a pair of our Dolce and Banana underwear.

"No ship," chimed in Carson from the office next door.

I nodded. "Ship yeah."

"Holy ship!" swore Carson.

"Yeah, Savannah Bananas free shipping," I sagely added.

Patrick walked in, curious. "Who gives a ship?"

Lizzy, Director of Merchandise, enlightened him, "I give a ship. All the time and for free."

"Wow! I may just ship my underwear!" Patrick exclaimed.

I ship you not, that was a fun commercial to make. And it served two goals: we got to promote our new line of Dolce and Banana underwear and announce that we had eliminated all shipping costs (gotta get rid of that friction).

There's no reason announcements need to be boring. The best message is always the most entertaining one. How do we know? Because after I told the world that I shipped my underwear, we now sell shiploads of underwear all over the world. No ship!

Normal marketing gets normal results. Entertaining marketing gets remarkable results. And make no mistake, even your invoices can be remarkable. If you get a bill from the Bananas, here's what it will say:

> Congrats. This is your day, the day you've been waiting for. Today's the day you get to pay. You may think you've had days like this—the day you bought your first house, the day you bought your first car, or maybe your first all-inclusive vacation. Nothing is quite like Bananas payday.
>
> So pull out your money order, savings bond, Bitcoin, gold, cash, credit card, check, and make that payment like we

know you can. We believe in you. This is your moment. Now seize it. Your life will never be the same.

Love, the Savannah Bananas.

P.S. It's now time to sit back, relax, and sip on a Slippery Banana. Your dreams are about to come true.

If you were on the receiving end of that invoice, how would you feel? Sure, you'd still have to give up some of your money, but at least you'd get to have fun doing it.

And that's the point. Entertaining is worth it just for entertainment's sake, but it's also a friction fighter's favorite tool. It helped us eliminate the friction of shipping costs and the awkward friction of sending and receiving invoices. The more you go all-in, the more you commit to having fun, the more you eliminate friction points and give others permission to have fun too.

Attend to the Details

"Do what you do so well that they will want to come back and bring their friends."

—WALT DISNEY

Merchandise Director Lizzy Mackerty joined the Bananas as a plant. Not a banana plant. A Bananas plant. She was there at the big name reveal in February 2016, cheering loudly alongside Jared's wife, Kelsey, to help us build the hype.

By watching her performance, you never would have known that Lizzy secretly didn't like the name Bananas. She thought we picked it just because it rhymed! Luckily, the name grew on her, and quickly Lizzy went from plant to merch master.

Lizzy will be the first to tell you that her first day on the job was a bit overwhelming. The Bananas were getting national attention, and we weren't ready to handle the surge of merch orders that came with that attention. "We had a little table with printed Excel sheets of orders taped together, five down and six across," Lizzy remembers. "We used a ruler and a highlighter to keep track of each fan's line of information."

Our packing and mailing operation was equally disorganized. Let's just say that when they saw us come through their doors, the lovely workers at the local post office were not entertained.

Lizzy knew we could do better, and she took it upon herself to make it happen. What could we do to make our merch process Fans First? How could we create an experience from the moment a fan thought about ordering merchandise to the moment they got it? What would make it easy? What would make it fun? What would make it unique?

Lizzy decided that merch and shipping could be just as much of a stage as the field at Grayson. So she helped turn the experience into its own little sideshow.

The merch script starts with a confirmation email:

> Congrats! You just made the best decision of your day. Just now, as your order came in, the entire staff celebrated with

a parade around Grayson Stadium. After numerous songs, dances, high-fives, and Gatorade showers, we were hoisting your items into the air. There is maximum security, including twenty-four-hour surveillance, and your order will be taken care of right away. It'll be mailed to you first class. Now, sit back, relax, and mentally prepare for the best purchase of your life with the Savannah Bananas. Go Bananas!

Lizzy also included a section on our order form where a fan can leave a personal note for the order: "Happy anniversary!" or "Congrats on the new baby!" That way, when we see these notes, we'll include something extra related to the note, like a onesie.

Then, the team puts the merchandise in yellow boxes stamped "Delivered Fresh" with yellow tissue paper and a free decal and foam can cooler. They include a message printed on yellow paper decorated with a fun explosion and Lizzy's contact info, saying:

It's here! Your official Bananas gear. Every item is personally handled with care, wrapped in our bright yellow tissue paper, and delivered fresh to you. All of our Bananas merchandise is sprinkled with potassium and topped with awesomeness. We personally guarantee all of your friends will be jealous. Show off your Bananas gear to the world by tagging #gobananas. Who knows? Your pic could go viral! Welcome to the bunch.

There are a few other details to the show, but needless to say, the merch script is a much more sophisticated operation than the old fly-by-your-pants approach we took in the early days.

More importantly, it's fun—and it creates fans in ways we never would have expected.

Just ask Gerry, the biggest Bananas fan who has never actually been to Savannah or a Bananas game (at least, not by the time we finished this book). An older gentleman who lives part time in Florida, Gerry saw someone wearing our merch one day and immediately wanted to know more about us.

So he called Lizzy up (remember that prominent phone number on our website?), began asking her a bunch of questions, and finally settled on his first merch order: a neon green T-shirt. The day Gerry's package arrived, Lizzy got another phone call. Gerry couldn't believe the attention to detail, from the box to all the extras. He was so excited that he ordered a dozen more pieces of merch for all his friends because, as he said, they were all asking for the can coolers!

Even though he has never been to a Bananas show, Gerry keeps ordering merch, and Lizzy keeps finding new ways to entertain him. She even included a voucher for free tickets to a game for Gerry and his wife—reserved seats—so the couple could *really* experience what the Bananas are all about.

COVID-19 put a hold on Gerry's first Bananas game, but as luck would have it, we bumped into him at Disney World during a staff trip just before COVID-19 hit.

"I saw this man approach us with his neon green T-shirt and new Bananas navy blue hat with the green brim. I'm like, 'That's Gerry. It's gotta be him,'" Lizzy remembers.

Gerry was over the moon to see and meet everybody, finally, in person, after a year and a half of phone calls. And he was even more interested in the military-themed Bananas shirt one of our team members was wearing. He was bummed to learn they were no longer available, but Lizzy wasn't going to leave it at that. Secretly, for his next birthday, Lizzy called our vendor and had a military-style shirt specially printed for him with his name and the number five, for his birthdate, on the back.

When Gerry got the shirt, he called Lizzy up, ecstatic. "How'd you know what my number was?" Happenstance had created serendipity; the number five was Gerry's old college number.

I'll say it again. Every touchpoint is a stage, a chance to create an unforgettable experience. By attending to the details in the merch department and by writing a script that always put fans first, Lizzy created a family of lifelong fans.

Thank Me? No, Thank *You!*

"Good morning! I just wanted to send a thank you your way! I received a call yesterday. Turns out, it was the Savannah Bananas calling to thank me for ordering tickets. How amazing is that? Your team goes above and beyond in every aspect of customer service and entertainment. We are taking off work and traveling over five

*hours just to go to the game, and we couldn't be more
excited that we actually got tickets. So thank you to all
the players and the staff. We can't wait to see you!"*

—CRISTY FARROW WATSON, BANANAS FAN

Push the Fun Envelope

*"It's always fun. It didn't even feel like work, being
around the stadium and seeing your fans and all
the workers, and there are parades, music, and
dancers. We're just watching baseball, and then
you get free snacks and everything. So it doesn't feel
like work at all."*

—COLTON, BANANAS HIGH-FIVER

If you're having fun, push it a little further, right to the edge of
"too far." You'll find that it's not as dangerous or scary as you
think.

You might think the opposing team and their fans are off-limits
here. Wrong. If we're really going all-in with Fans First, we want
to go all-in for *all* fans who come to our ballpark.

After all, they may be your opponent's fans today, but they could
be your fans tomorrow.

130 | FANS FIRST

Sometimes when we introduce the visiting lineup, someone on staff dresses as the Grim Reaper. A staff member puts on a Grim Reaper costume, walks over to the dugout (complete with theme music), and stares down at the visiting players. It's morbid, but you remember it. This gag ultimately kick-started a whole slew of unique, funny introductions for the visiting team.

Because we can't let anything be normal, even the other team.

We keep the fun going from there with our "donut hitters." When a visiting hitter strikes out, all the fans get free donuts. The donut hitter is announced ahead of time, so as soon as he comes to bat, the entire stadium starts chanting "donuts, donuts" in hopes that guy strikes out.

You'd think maybe this would be one of the worst experiences a batter could have in his life. For some, maybe it is. But a lot of the visiting players get into it, tipping their hats to the fans after they fan out because, hey, at least they got everyone free donuts. Might as well own it.

Some opposing players take owning it seriously. After a playoff game during our 2021 championship season, two of the visiting players walked into our merch store and bought Bananas gear on their way out. It was something I never thought I'd see in my life. Imagine a Yankees player losing to the Red Sox in the playoffs but making sure he got some Red Sox gear before he left the ballpark. Crazy. But I guess even our visitors are inspired to push the fun envelope when we do.

By bringing the opposing team into the show, by entertaining *them*, too, we make ourselves a new set of fans. We've had several players from opposing teams join our premier team during the offseason because they want to be a part of what we're doing. Once they join up, they all say the same thing: there's nothing like playing in Savannah.

My Way

"We were leaving at the end of the night, after visiting with the players on the field, walking through the concourse to the front gates. Ricardo Maldonado (then known to us as Cam) was mopping up a section where something had spilled and singing 'My Way' by Frank Sinatra. The almost empty hallway provided the perfect acoustics for his deeply sonorous voice, and my husband joined him. I wish I had thought to pull my camera out, but I just stood there and listened, enjoying just another magical Banana memory."

—JENNIFER MAY, BANANAS FAN

Turn Your Limits into Strengths

"Empty pockets never held anyone back. Only empty heads and empty hearts can do that."

—NORMAN VINCENT PEALE

Darren Ross is the COO of Magic Castle Hotel in Hollywood. Built in 1957, Magic Castle isn't exactly the modern, amenity-filled experience that modern travelers are used to. As Darren says, "We don't have an elevator. We don't have a bar. We don't have a restaurant. We don't have room service. We don't have a gym. We don't have a spa. There are a lot of things we don't have that are part of our story."

There is one thing they do have: Darren. And he knows that even with all these limitations, he can still find ways to entertain his guests.

To make Magic Castle a one-of-a-kind experience, Darren drew from his own childhood traveling experiences. He couldn't control what they didn't have, but he could create a happy, nostalgic experience full of 1950s charm.

First, they added a free snack bar filled with every kid's dream: potato chips, pretzels, popcorn, granola bars, and full-size candy bars. Then, they added a free DVDs menu, a free laundry service, a free beverage bar, and a free soft-serve ice-cream machine— where visiting kids get to choose the flavor for the day.

For me, though, the best part of the Magic Castle experience was the free popsicle hotline.

This ingenious idea started with poolside service on silver trays a few times a day and grew into a red phone mounted on the wall right by the pool that calls directly to the front desk. If someone picks up that phone, they receive an array of delicious popsicles, stat. Guests take their pictures with them. Kids search for the phone on check-in. As Darren says, "It's playful. It's fun. It's inexpensive for us. It's a conversation piece, and people are talking about it."

This is how scripting can help control the context. With fun waiting around every corner, guests don't focus on the facility. They focus on the value and uniqueness of the experience.

Also, it saves Magic Castle tons in marketing costs. Darren doesn't need to spend a lot to advertise. His guests do it for him through tons of repeat business and referrals. That's how Magic Castle can keep its occupancy rate in the nineties—something unheard of for a small, independent hotel from another era.

If you want that Magic Castle magic, look at what assets you have, and ask how you can use them to entertain your future fans and create a better experience. It doesn't have to be big—just thoughtful.

Script the Feeling

Focusing on fun is only one way to create a feeling for your fans. If you're the Ritz Carlton, for instance, then you're going for a different feeling—calm, elegant, sophisticated, tranquil.

The exact feeling you create is up to you, but you're only going to create it if you think it through in advance. What feeling do you want *your* fans to experience when they interact with your business? How are you going to script your touchpoints to create this feeling?

Entertain Even When You Can't

"If you wait for certainty, you will spend your whole life standing still."

—KEVIN HART

Entertaining always means entertaining, even in the most challenging and unexpected of circumstances. Remember, scripting gives you control of the experience, so it's important to grab control when you feel the most out of control.

In the early days of the COVID-19 pandemic, like everyone else, the Savannah Bananas shut down. Everyone was at home. No one knew if there was going to be a season. But as long as we still had jobs, we had a job to do: entertain.

The ballpark might have been closed, but we weren't shutting down for the fans. We had to find ways to entertain our fans while they were at home—to do what we do best, but in a way we'd never done before.

First things first: Ideapalooza. In addition to informal idea sessions, we also have Ideapaloozas every couple of months. We take the team somewhere offsite (and with alcohol), and we let the ideas flow until we're all tapped out. In the case of COVID-19, offsite became a rather weird Zoom call (weird because some took it upon themselves to dress in costume) where everyone contributed ideas to help us figure out how to entertain outside of the ballpark. Some ideas were absolutely ridiculous, and some were pure gold. We wanted it all.

Some of the ideas were no-brainers. We were already known for our music videos, so it was only natural that we take this moment to create a new one. Given that we were all in quarantine, Billy Idol's song "Dancing with Myself" felt like the natural pick. Everyone on the team recorded a lip-sync montage of themselves dancing around to the song at their house, using plungers and other objects as microphones and props.

Next, we sent an email out to our fans, asking them to get in on the fun and share their best videos from home. We compiled all the clips together, set them to the tune of "Hey Baby," and turned our fans into stars.

My favorite quarantine idea was a show we broadcasted on Facebook live, *Cooking with Bananas*. Every week, a different team member welcomed the world into their home and did their best Julia Child impression. Although, instead of cooking photo-perfect French delicacies, we stumbled through even simple recipes like macaroni and cheese.

Emily and I took turns as hosts of the show, too, and it was a beautiful disaster. Our son, Maverick, who was about two at the time, had his own agenda that night...and it didn't involve cooking. The meal was a wash, but the realness of trying to cook with a toddler still made the night a hit.

Eventually, after a lot of collaboration with health professionals and the city, we were able to play a shortened, socially distanced season in 2020. Rainouts may have hurt us in the past, but in this new pandemic environment, we were so grateful to have an outdoor facility. When the fans returned to Grayson Stadium, they thanked us for being there for them during a time when everyone was shut off and isolated. We thanked them for showing back up to the games and keeping the magic of Bananaland alive.

Always means always. Entertain your fans, even when you can't. Find ways to stay involved and connected.

MAKE THE NORMAL REMARKABLE

"I think I have learned that the best way to lift oneself up is to help someone else."

—BOOKER T. WASHINGTON

If your goal is to be part of your fans' lives—to be the remarkable thing they always talk about—then you must entertain always. Every touchpoint, from beginning to end. Build this into your mission, vision, and values.

This is serious business. If you aren't entertaining your fans, soon you won't have fans to entertain.

Find your boring and normal moments. Script them. How can these be made remarkable? How can you make something special for each type of fan, from the youngest to the oldest? Making good memories for your fans will balance out any small expense you incur, as your fans will become your most ardent and valuable marketers and repeat customers.

Look at your assets and spaces. Don't work from a mindset of what you lack; go with a mindset of what you have. What makes you unique? What *can* make you unique? Amplify that.

You don't have to go so far as throwing objects at your teammates' nanners. In fact, unless that teammate is all-in on the idea, I really wouldn't recommend it—and I'm sure your HR team wouldn't either. All you want is for your fans to feel, to be touched by something you did, to know that you see them as a *person*, not as a transaction.

When you stop entertaining, you stop caring. You stop feeling like people matter. You stop seeing each person's humanity.

So don't stop entertaining. Always keep at it. Listen to them. Lift them up. Show them that they matter.

Even during the worst of times. *Especially* during the worst of times.

The Bananas Bookshelf

All Business Is Show Business: Strategies for Earning Standing Ovations from Your Customers by Scott McKain

Dream It! Do It! My Half Century Creating Disney's Magic Kingdoms by Marta Sklar

THE 2ND-INNING STRETCH

"If anyone's depressed for any reason, whether a relationship has fallen apart or they're having money problems, wearing feathered wings and a tutu takes you into a whole other world. A whole new woooooorld, a world of bright and shining stars!"

—RICHARD SIMMONS

It's about seven thirty. A visiting player has just struck out (free donuts, anyone?) for the third out. Their half of the inning is over, and the Bananas trot off the field.

And then someone with curly hair and '80s-era spandex comes running out.

"Is that...Richard Simmons?" a fan asks.

It is. Or at least a Richard Simmons lookalike. And he's about to get the crowd pumped up.

"Okay, people. Everyone on their feet!" the pseudo-Simmons bellows into the mic. "Let's stretch those limbs out."

The fans don't know what's going on, but they play along. After all, it *is* a Bananas game, so a surprise second-inning stretch makes its own kind of sense.

Simmons continues to lead the party, leading the fans through a variety of thrusts, gyrations, and dances that most of their bodies aren't accustomed to doing. A few people stay seated, sticking out like a bruised banana.

And then just like that, the pseudo-Simmons is gone. The visiting team takes the field, and the Bananas take their turn at bat.

So why do we have second-inning stretches instead of seventh-inning stretches? Because whatever's normal, we do the exact opposite. We've got to keep the show rolling. We don't want people to think they've settled into a normal ballgame. Nothing entertaining about that.

In fact, while we're here, why don't you take a moment to stand up, stretch, and shake your limbs out too? Yes, I'm talking to you. Don't make me sic pseudo-Simmons on you.

Okay, feeling better? Are you still with us? Ready to dial things up a little more?

Good. Because now the show is really about to get wild.

From here on out, I'm going to be flinging ideas and stories at you like you just told me you were all-in for a Bananas promotion video.

This is the point of no return.

If you're not all-in, if you prefer to sit, that's okay too. Just pass this book along to another dancer.

3rd Inning

EXPERIMENT CONSTANTLY

"We keep moving forward, opening new doors, and doing new things because we're curious. And curiosity keeps leading us down new paths. We're always exploring and experimenting."

—WALT DISNEY

It was the first night of our One City World Tour. As part of the pregame show, we decided to borrow a page out of the boxing playbook and have all our players weigh in.

Jared played the role of the announcer, complete in a black suit and bowtie. We rolled out the scale—a big, old-school device we found at an antique store.

"Ladies and gentlemen, it's time for our official weigh-in!" Jared began.

Or at least, that's what I think he said. Honestly, you couldn't hear him over the marching band parading through the grandstands. But since his mic had cut out anyway, I guess it didn't matter.

The parade of errors continued. The players lined up in the wrong place. Then the scale didn't work. We had to guess all the players' weights like carnies.

You could say the first weigh-in did not go as planned, but we got the hang of it. Now that the weigh-ins are a little more established, the players get into it. One of our players once approached the scale and proceeded to rip off his jersey—and then his undershirt. He told us he was 270 pounds of pure muscle, and we had no reason to doubt it. The crowd went nuts.

One of the players from our premier team, the Party Animals, showed up in a leather jacket—which he then proceeded to rip off, revealing his very drawn-on six-pack abs. Another wore a jean jacket with the sleeves cut off, along with a pair of women's Daisy Duke shorts underneath. Still another player walked up in only Dolce and Banana underwear, which, since he was ripped like Captain America, he pulled off to perfection.

Did this bit get off to a rocky start? Sure, but that's usually how our experiments go the first time we run through them. We look at what worked and what didn't, do what we can to fix the bugs, and then try again the next night.

Experimenting isn't about getting it right. It's about trying something new. It's about pushing what's possible.

Everything is about the experience. What are your customers saying when they experience your product? Are they saying anything? A lot of companies don't try new things. They do the same thing over and over again. That creates boredom—another one of our four-letter words. So we experiment.

Most businesses experiment with some aspect of their business every now and then. We experiment constantly. Sometimes we fail, and then we learn. As Bananas Finance Director Matt Powell says, "Our company encourages experiments so much that you feel guilty *not* trying something new each game. But the coolest thing is that if it doesn't work, that's okay. We now know to try something else new. But if it does work, that's an opportunity to really have a big impact on our fans."

If you want to keep having the same impact on your fans, keep doing the same thing. If you want to keep creating an even greater impact, then it's up to you to keep experimenting. In this chapter, we're going to show you the mad laboratory where we cook up all our wildest experiments and create unforgettable experiences.

CREATING A CULTURE OF EXPERIMENTATION

"A person who never made a mistake never tried anything new."

—ALBERT EINSTEIN

If you ever got an F in school, you probably didn't like the feeling. No one does. But where some people turn that F into a lot of other bad F-words—like *fear* or *failure*—the Bananas see that F as a learning opportunity. Rather than being driven by fear, we're driven by the joy of constantly creating new, engaging experiences for our fans.

Jon Spoelstra, author and former president of NBA teams like the Buffalo Braves, Portland Trail Blazers, Denver Nuggets, and New Jersey Nets, regularly talks about creating a culture of experimentation, or what he calls "making new a way of life."

For many of the new staff and interns, our freewheeling, experimenting ways are a new way of life. In most areas of life, we're not encouraged to try new things. With the Bananas, it's mandatory—and it starts right away.

Just ask Austin the Awkward Rapper.

We do everything we can to welcome all our new team members, including interns, on their first day and make them feel as included as possible. We also like to throw them into the deep end (supervised, of course), so Emily and I invited Austin to share any ideas he had for the team. That's step one to building a culture of experimentation: creating the context. If you want your team to give you ideas, then give them the opportunity.

Austin said he loved the thank-you calls we made when fans bought tickets or merch. "But they're kinda boring," he said.

That got my attention. "What do you think we should do to make them better?"

"Why not make them raps?" he said without missing a beat.

"Perfect. By the end of the day, you'll do a thank-you rap call," I said with a big grin on my face.

That's step two to building a culture of experimentation. Don't just have your team share ideas. Have them implement their ideas too. ASAP.

But expect resistance. Austin tried backtracking almost immediately, explaining he was socially awkward and uncomfortable with that type of thing. I told him that would just make the call even more perfect. He'd be Austin the Awkward Bananas Rapper, a one-of-a-kind source of entertainment.

That convinced him.

Austin spent the next four hours drafting his rap. It was his sole job for the day. Every time we checked in on him, he was out-of-his-mind nervous and a little red-faced. Finally, four o'clock rolled around. Time to get on the phone and make that call.

"You're gonna do great," I said as we handed him the banana phone.

Visibly shaking, he dialed a recent merch buyer's number. Then, Austin let rip with a phat flow: "Hey, this is Austin the Awkward Bananas Rapper. I'm here to fill your day with fun, joy, and laughter. I hope you enjoy your merch. Thank you so much for this awesome perch..." and so on.

Soon, Austin finished his rap. The fan thanked him for the call, and that was that.

Austin put down the phone and looked at me, beaming. "Hey, it wasn't that bad!"

"Of course it wasn't!" I said.

And just like that, a legend was born. Every day for the entire time he was with us, Austin the Awkward Rapper would thrill fans with his lovable raps. Sometimes, fans would call us up just so they could hear a fresh Austin rhyme.

Experimenting is often scary at first. Even I'm scared when we roll out a lot of our experiments—especially the big ones like our inaugural One City World Tour in Mobile in 2021. But here's the thing: the worst thing that may happen is never as bad as what you imagine could happen.

The biggest mistake is not making any.

The quicker you can go from the idea to the event, the less time you have to worry about it. That's why, just like with Austin, whenever a team member has an idea, we ask them to come up with a plan to implement it that same day.

Quick implementation also teaches a culture of empowerment (more on this later). Essentially, you're saying, "We want you to do this because we believe in you, and we believe in this idea. We trust you to run with this." It can be as small as writing a rap for a fan or as large as changing an existing practice (or initiating a new one).

This brings us to step three for building a culture of empowerment: be giving with both your time and your money so your team has the room to experiment.

Companies like 3M and Google have adopted what is known as the 20 percent rule, where their people are encouraged to spend 20 percent of their time on a project of their own initiative and choosing. Taking this concept one step further, 3M also has a 30 percent rule, where each division is expected to generate thirty percent of their annual sales from products and services that have been introduced in the past five years. They also have Genesis Grants, an internal venture capital fund that awards up to $50,000 for researchers to develop prototypes in market tests.

Our annual budget isn't as big as 3M's or Google's, but we now allocate 1 percent of it for experiments. If someone has an idea for an experiment that will cost money, we'll fund it. Through these practices, we show our team that we don't just encourage experimentation; we expect it.

Reward Experimentation

In a culture of resting on your laurels, people are hesitant to scrap what they've always done. They don't want to get rid of what has worked for them in the past.

Even if something is still working, it may be time to get rid of it before it becomes obsolete. Try something new. We push this ideology in our culture. We ask what experiments each teammate is working on to create a great fan experience because that's what we value. We now give awards for the best experiment of the year.

How can you encourage and reward your team for experimentation?

EMBRACE THE MESS

"Keep throwing darts at the dartboard. You'll eventually hit the bull's-eye."

—WILL FERRELL

We're always borrowing ideas from different sports. We've borrowed the weigh-in from boxing. We've borrowed caddies from golf. We've even borrowed the halftime show from football (in our opinion, everything deserves a halftime show). Some of it works, and some of it doesn't.

One time our borrowing ways didn't work was when we decided to host a horse race between innings. We pulled a handful of kids from the stands, gave them horse masks, and had them take their marks. Then, they were off. One horse-headed kid trotted into second base. One pranced toward the pitcher's mound, and one galloped all the way to right field—they were all over the place.

Here's something you might not know: kids can't see a thing in a horse mask. And with nary a jockey in sight to guide these blinkered steeds, they all just kind of pointed themselves in the direction they thought they should go and took off.

Here's another thing you might not know: kids can't hear a thing in a horse mask either. They were running deaf and blind, with a very flustered dude in a yellow tuxedo chasing after them.

Yes, folks, I'm sorry to say, but I broke character that night—and everyone listening in on the livestream got to hear it.

I imagine it was quite a thing to watch. I was yelling at a bunch of horse-faced kids while they ran around, oblivious to everything. I know Jared certainly got a kick out of it, as he recounted the night's festivities in excruciating detail later on.

Back on the field, though, it didn't feel so fun. All I could think about was how big of a delay we were causing. Finally, we corralled all the kids. And as I trotted back into the dugout, the players gave me a warm round of applause.

Nothing about that promotion was fun, at least not for me. But if you asked me to do it again, I'd do it in a heartbeat.

Why? Because I know a secret: people don't remember your failures. They remember your successes.

Reggie Jackson is a baseball legend. He's Mr. October, author of some of the most epic moments in playoff history, like his three home runs in Game 6 of the 1977 World Series. He's a Hall of Famer, for crying out loud. He's also the career record holder for the most strikeouts, with a whopping 2,597 whiffs over a twenty-one-year career. But he's not known for his strikeouts; he's known for his hits.

Amazon is an unstoppable force in the consumer product world. They have Prime. They have Alexa. They even have drones that can deliver your mail. But one of the most successful companies of all time is also the developer of the Fire Phone—a clunker of a device that cost them millions of dollars in development and marketing. But the technology they innovated to develop the failed phone helped create Alexa.

I could go on, but you get the point.

Why sweat the failures when we have so many wins to celebrate? Why look down on failure when it often leads to success?

Experimentation is messy business. But it's how you get better. If you know how something is going to turn out before you try it, then it's not an experiment. It's a sure thing. And where's the fun in that?

All the best comics know this. Often, legends like Chris Rock or Jerry Seinfeld show up unexpectedly to a small comedy club to test new material. Unsurprisingly, that new material gets mixed results. Such is the nature of experimenting—they're learning what material does and doesn't work.

It would be easy for the Chris Rocks and Jerry Seinfelds of the world to stick to the big stages and the big tours, using only the material that always works. However, they know that if they did that, they'd be doing it for the money rather than for the fans.

The same goes for the Bananas. If we did the exact same promotion for every game, in every new city, we wouldn't be pushing ourselves for our fans. We would become stale and irrelevant.

That's why we commit to experimenting with, at minimum, four new promotions every night. Something new in pregame, something new in the game, a new hitting entrance, and a new scoring celebration. Most of them don't go as planned, but we usually find one gem every game that makes a huge impact.

Hit or horse race, we have to try. It's the only way to discover.

Besides, if things go *really* bad (we've certainly had more epic failures than a horse race), we can always just change tack. That's why we have what we call "swings" built into our scripts. If a promotion isn't coming together or there's some type of delay or problem, we drop it and swing to something else instead.

But whatever happens, we embrace the mess of the moment and learn how to make the show better the next night.

Read All Bad Reviews,
But Don't Worry About Them

Banana ball: It's an absolute joke. I came to see base-ball. This is not baseball. This is fake baseball.

All-you-can-eat tickets: they aren't great when the food is inedible.

Bananas Insiders: At five bucks a month, what an absolute waste of money. Might as well just light my money on fire.

These are actual reviews that fans have left, and they aren't the only bad reviews we've gotten. It comes with the territory of experimentation (it also comes with the territory of normalcy, so take your pick what you want to be booed for).

Good or bad, I want people to think and say something. If you are not getting criticized, you are playing it too safe. And even a bad review can help you improve.

But it takes courage to read bad reviews. To get past the criticism, you have to become a fan of yourself. Have fun. If you're having fun, you can't get lost in the negative.

LEARN FROM DOING

"Failures are the most important product."

—RW JOHNSON

Southwest Airlines co-founder Herb Kelleher was famous for saying, "Do, then learn." Since we do a lot, the Bananas learn a lot.

Sometimes, like with the horse races, we learn what not to do. I love it when that happens. The more we learn what not to do, the more we learn what we're good at.

For instance, in the early years, we hosted a lot of non-baseball-related events at Grayson Stadium:

- Running of the Bananas

- Ghosts of Grayson Haunted Stadium

- Tap of the Morning Beer Festival

- Field of Food Trucks

Each of these events brought its share of challenges and successes. We had a lot of fun putting these events on and seeing our fans' reactions, but something was nagging at me: what business were we in? Were we really operating in our sweet spot? Were we really giving our fans what they wanted?

Our moment of clarity came when we decided to host Jimmy Buffett tribute bands as the centerpiece of our Bananas Beach Bash. We set it up, printed up tons of shirts, and tried to hype it up as best as we could.

We only sold three hundred tickets. Then, when it looked like a hurricane was going to blow through town the day of the concert, we decided to cancel the event.

The hurricane never came. After paying out the band and promoters and shipping the unused T-shirts to the fans who had bought tickets, we took a long, hard look at the types of events we were putting on at Grayson Stadium.

The people who came out to these events weren't necessarily Bananas fans, and the events themselves weren't on-brand. It was good to experiment and say yes to all of our crazy ideas in the beginning, but the more we started to find our sweet spot, the more we realized that these events weren't what our fans wanted. They wanted excellent Bananas games.

What a great lesson.

We didn't need the other events. Bananas games *were* the event. Once we understood this, we began experimenting like crazy *within* our sweet spot, rolling these external shows into the one we already had. Instead of hosting a separate Oktoberfest, for instance, we had the idea for an Oktoberfest-themed game, complete with lederhosen! Sadly, COVID-19 shutdowns put a delay on this particular event, but it started a whole chain of similar holiday-themed events for Halloween, Thanksgiving (Fansgiving), and Christmas.

By learning what we weren't good at, we also learned how to make what we *were* good at even better—specifically, making baseball more fun.

GO BIG OR GO HOME: THE GAME-CHANGING EXPERIMENT

"We're actively looking for new cliffs to jump off. We're doing things that nobody else will do because they can't chase us into those spaces. We didn't get here by playing the rules of the game. We got here by setting the rules of the game."

—CHRIS ALBRECHT, FORMER CHAIRMAN AND CEO OF HBO

Many well-known companies of today found success through experimenting. Marriott was a food and beverage company before it branched out into the hotel business. Johnson and Johnson originally sold zero consumer goods. IBM and HP had no experience with computers when they launched their first computer products.

You must constantly invent to create fans. When you rest on your laurels and stop inventing, you are irrelevant. You don't matter anymore. Complacency (read: normalcy) is why failed businesses fail.

That's why, in 2020, we introduced the world to a whole new brand of baseball.

When the Savannah Bananas play games as part of the independent Coastal Plain League, we play by the traditional rules of baseball. But when we play exhibitions in the spring and fall as a premier, paid professional team, it's a whole new ballgame.

We call it Banana Ball.

The idea for Banana Ball began in 2018. For three years, the Bananas had done everything they could to build the best hot dog stand around, but we were still selling hot dogs. In other words, the baseball game we played on the field was still long, slow, and boring.

It was time to sell a better hot dog. We had to change the game of baseball itself.

This was a big experiment—the biggest we'd ever attempted up to that point. We got to work right away, but we took our time with the result. For the next two years, we developed and tested a brand-new version of baseball, tossing out old rules we didn't like and inserting new rules in their place.

Finally, we settled on nine new rules that would transform how the game was played:[7]

1. **Every inning counts.** The team that scores the most runs in an inning gets a point. The inning is over once the home team takes the lead or three outs are recorded against the home team. This shortens the

---

7 "Banana Ball Rules," Savannah Bananas, https://thesavannahbananas.com/banana-ball-rules/.

game. You can play a whole nine-inning game in nine-ty-nine minutes. And fans are on the edge of their seats the whole time.

2. **Two-hour time limit.** No inning will start after the two-hour point. If the game is tied at the end of two hours, it will go into a showdown to determine the winner. This also ensures a shorter game.

3. **No stepping out.** Batters cannot step out of the batter's box once an at-bat starts. If the batter steps out at any point, it's a strike. Another elimination of wasted time.

4. **No bunting.** Bunting sucks. If a batter bunts, he will be thrown out of the game. Get that nonsense out of here.

5. **Batters can steal first.** If a passed ball or wild pitch happens during any pitch of an at-bat, the batter can take off for first.

6. **No walks allowed.** If a pitcher throws a fourth ball, it becomes a sprint. The hitter sprints to first while the defense has to throw the ball to every player on the field before they can throw the runner out. The hitter advances as many bases as he can. The ball does not have to touch the catcher or the pitcher. More running = less boring.

7. **One-on-one showdown tiebreaker.** Each team picks one pitcher and one hitter to face off. The defensive team only has the pitcher, a single fielder,

and the catcher on the field. If a hitter puts the ball in play, he has to make it home to get a point. The pitcher and fielder are allowed to chase the ball and throw the ball to the catcher for a play at the plate. If a pitcher strikes the batter out or gets him out before scoring, he doesn't get a point. If the batter walks, he can take second base, and the hitting team brings another hitter to the plate. If the score is tied, the first team to keep the other team from scoring wins. This adds the heightened stakes that soccer and hockey have in their shootouts and sudden-death overtimes.

8. **No mound visits.** Let's keep the game moving. No mound visits from the coach, catcher, or any other players. Hype your pitcher up from afar if needed.

9. **If a fan catches a foul ball, it's an out.** Why not let the fans get in on some of the action? People bring ball gloves to games for a reason. It's the best rule—it's what every kid has always dreamed about. Think of the media interviewing a kid because they helped win the game. Think of the choice you make as a fan *not* to catch a foul ball to help your team. Now that's high drama! (Fun fact: the first fan foul ball catch was made by an adult who caught a foul ball hit by a Banana. When that out was recorded, the fan was booed.)

The first time we played Banana Ball live, we had the pleasure of playing in front of two thousand kids. It was an intersquad game, green Bananas versus yellow Bananas.

Like all experiments, that first game came with some hiccups—especially because we had no real way of communicating the rules to the fans without a jumbotron. Even the players got confused at first. The very first play in front of people was an inside-the-park home run/walk. (If you're confused reading that, don't worry. I'm confused writing it.) The player had to sprint his walk, and since the opposing players forgot Rule #6, he was able to run all the way home.

Hiccups aside, I knew we had done something magical that day. For the first time in a long time, we had made baseball a living, breathing thing again.

Now, all we had to do was check in with our young fans to see if this experiment worked. It did. The kids and their counselors loved it. Kids who weren't even baseball fans were raving about the quick pace and how much fun the game was to watch. The only suggestion they had was to create two different teams instead of a green squad and a yellow squad. Thus, the Party Animals were born.

Finally, we had a new hot dog—and it tasted like Bananas.

It took a lot of nanners to change the game. It also created a lot of noise. After debuting Banana Ball, the Bananas were featured in the *Boston Globe*, the *Chicago Morning News*, and even *The Wall Street Journal*.

Did we turn off some traditional baseball fans in the process? Yes, but that's okay. There's plenty of long, slow, and boring baseball out there for them to enjoy.

In the meantime, we've kept pushing the envelope. All Banana Ball games end at nine o'clock because everyone goes home then anyway. Next, we'll be adding yellow baseballs (we already have yellow bases). Honestly, I'm surprised we haven't done that already.

From there, who knows? We'll probably start reaching out to the fans to hear what else they have to say and what rules they would change. We might even let them play. Talk about the ultimate fantasy league.

11...

Be a Game-Changer

Think about the rules of your business. What can you change to be more exciting and fan-friendly? How can you involve your fans more in rulemaking? Push the envelope. What rules would make you slightly uncomfortable to change but need to change to refresh your business and industry?

TREAT EVERY DAY LIKE DAY ONE

"Our success is a direct function of how many experiments we do per year, per month, per week, per day."

—JEFF BEZOS

10...

There's no greater company at experimenting than Amazon. Say what you want about Jeff Bezos. I know he's created a lot of controversies, but experimenting has been his driving force.

9...

If you read his 1997 shareholders letter, Bezos preached that every day is day one. Once they treat a day like it's day two, they die because that's the day they've stopped experimenting.

8...

When Bezos stepped down as CEO in 2021, he reemphasized his belief in experimentation. In his farewell letter to employees, he said, "Keep inventing, and don't despair when at first the idea looks crazy. Remember to wander. Let curiosity be your compass. It remains day one." When you stop inventing new things for your fans, you die. It's not just about entertaining and eliminating friction. You have to bring new things to life constantly.

7...

The hardest question I get asked is, "Can you tell me about your failures?" I never know how to answer it. I suppose you could see a lot of the stories in this book as failures. I just see them as input on what to do next.

6...

Don't dwell on what doesn't work. Take your lesson and move on. Create an experiment list. Keep trying new things. Quantity will lead to quality—the only way to learn more is to do more.

5...

I don't believe in failure. I believe in discovery. The quickest path to innovation is through discovery. The only way to discover is to constantly try new things. The more you try, the more you discover.

In other words, eliminate the word *failure* from your vocabulary. Failure is negative. It yells at you and tells you to never try again.

4...

Rather than calling them failures, call them discoveries. Or call them swings like we do—or "going off script" like Disney does.

3...

An experiment is just that—an experiment. It's not an experiment if you know that it's going to work perfectly. A real experiment could go wrong, *and that's okay*.

2...

An experiment is just the testing of a hypothesis, meaning there's a *chance* it will turn out the way you expect and a chance it won't. Either way, you get more data—which gets you closer to the goal.

1...

The Bananas don't ever approach an experiment with the mindset that it's not going to work. We approach it knowing it will lead us to something that does.

0!

The Bananas Bookshelf

Built to Last: Successful Habits of Visionary Companies by Jim Collins and Jerry I. Porras

Invent and Wander: The Collected Writings of Jeff Bezos by Jeff Bezos

THE HALFTIME SHOW

"My wife: I don't like baseball.

Also my wife: Bananas games are so fun!"

—CHASE MCGARITY, BANANAS FAN

It was March 13, 2021, right in the middle of our St. Patrick's Day game. The players were in their finest kilts. Everything was Irish-themed, and everyone was having a good time.

Without warning, a countdown began, starting from eleven (gotta keep it different here). No one knew what they were counting down to, but they were happy to go along with it as the players sprinted off the field.

The countdown hit zero. Everyone cheered. Then they waited to see what they were cheering about.

"Ladies and gentlemen," our announcer said, "it's time for our halftime show. Please welcome the Savannah Pipe and Drum Band!"

The crowd cheered again.

And then nothing.

Where was the band?

I was in the dugout panicking. Sure, we didn't get to rehearse this bit, but we *did* plan this cue with the band we'd hired. Last I saw them, stowed away in the locker room, they all seemed happy and ready to go.

And now they weren't coming out. How the Split did we lose a group of guys in kilts and holding drums and bagpipes? Even in our circus, that stood out.

Then I saw movement over by the dugout.

Finally, the small group of elders, ages ranging somewhere between sixty and eighty, ambled onto the field, kilts billowing in the summer breeze as their knobby knees kicked into gear. They made for quite a sight: tartans tarting up tired shoulders. Silvery sporrans swinging suggestively on chains. Bony hips flashing their flashy flashes.

At this point, I was in the dugout pacing back and forth, asking them to speed it up. This was on its way to becoming the slowest halftime show ever.

The band stayed stoic and silent as they arranged themselves into a small circle facing each other between the pitcher's mound and home plate. They didn't face the crowd (how was I supposed to know this was traditional positioning for small

Scottish pipe bands?). They didn't even acknowledge the fans. They just put pipes to lips and sticks to drums and played at each other like they were being judged by William Wallace himself.

All I could do was watch.

It was a bit weird.

And awkward.

And anticlimactic.

Even the umpire dancing a jig in the outfield couldn't save this bit.

Eventually, the bagpipers were all piped out, and the umpire returned to his position.

If that wasn't the longest two minutes ever for a Bananas game, it was certainly the strangest. Judging from their reactions, though, the fans seemed to like it just fine. That was the first and last halftime show of the 2021 season. It was a fun experiment, but we had some execution issues to work out before we tried it again.

But that's experimenting for you. You either get a win or you get a story.

If you like the idea, keep working on it until it comes together. Keep tweaking it until it's different enough, remarkable enough, or silly enough to work.

And if it never works, at the very least it probably opened the door to other new ideas—like putting the first-ever baseball halftime show in a book. No one's going to forget that.

4th Inning

ENGAGE DEEPLY

"Do for one what you wish you could do for many."

—ANDY STANLEY

Four-year Bananas veteran Kyle Luigs knows his favorite Fans First moment.

It was during one of our "salute to the military" nights. A child of a veteran himself, Kyle knew how much military families sacrifice when a parent is deployed, so these nights were always special to him. But this night in particular was especially meaningful.

On this night, we staged a bit of a bait and switch. To start the game, we brought a group of siblings onto the field for a small promotion. The kids' job was simple: to line up in a row and greet all the players as they emerged from the tunnel.

"They were so excited," Kyle remembers. "All they could think about was how they should greet all the players."

What they didn't know was that a surprise was waiting for them at the end of that tunnel.

After all the players emerged, Kyle positioned the kids so their backs were to the tunnel entrance. Then, the announcer called the last "starting player," and their dad, who had just returned home from deployment, ran up behind them and surprised the kids with a hug.

As Kyle says, he only played a small part in that moment, but he'll never forget what it was like to see their faces light up in pure joy.

Human connection is everything. Love is better than like. It's not about the number of followers, ticket sales, or customers through the door. It's about engaging deeply. It's about doing for one what you wish you could do for many.

Bananas to the balls and shipping your underwear are great. That's the bedrock of how we live up to our value of entertaining always. But behind even the silliest moments is our commitment to creating real human connection between our staff, our interns, our players, and our fans.

If you want fans to be there for you when you need them, then your job is to be there for them always. Here's how to do it.

CREATING A CULTURE OF CONNECTION

"Spend time with fans. Make them feel special, and be inspiring to everyone you meet out there."

—BILL LEROY, BANANAS' LEGEND

Bill LeRoy wasn't even supposed to be a Banana. His original contract was for one day. "I was lucky just to even be there," Bill says. "I felt like I should take advantage of the opportunity since it was just so much about chance."

The first time Bill heard Fans First, he thought it was just a pat phrase from a brochure. Then he saw what Fans First was like in action—and more importantly, what it meant to the fans.

He's now one of our biggest advocates of engaging deeply, regularly going out of his way to make a fan's day. Bill believes the secret is to make fans feel, "Hey, he's just like me, a normal guy out there having a good time." This humanizing of the players makes fans, especially kids, feel like being a star is within their reach. He wants to show the kids that if he can do it, they can do it too. Bill grew up in the small town of Dublin, Georgia, and was never recruited heavily out of high school. He chose the University of North Georgia and became a standout on their team.

One day, he got the call from Coach Gillum to join the Bananas as a conditional player, just there to fill in for opening night until our main roster player arrived. All he had to do was put on a uniform and watch the game from the dugout before heading back to his hometown. He made it his goal to bring energy and do everything that was asked of him while he could.

So there Bill was—game one, ready to go. Well, okay, maybe not totally ready to go. Bill showed up without his cleats on and didn't think to check the lineup card.

Just as he was kicking back to soak up a good time, someone shouted at him.

"Hey, they need you behind the center field wall."

"What?" Bill said.

"You're in the starting nine," the person said. "They're waiting for you back there."

Bill threw his cleats on and scrambled out to center field, where he was greeted by another surprise—a big tank-like vehicle with a police escort. Around it, all the Bananas players were wearing SWAT-style helmets and hyping themselves up to make their grand entrance on the field. As Bill told me later, "I was in shock to be participating in all of this!"

The rest of the night brought shock after shock. Bill's first walk-up music. Bill's first crowd of more than a hundred people. Bill's first base hit (and Bill's second base hit). Bill's first win with the Bananas.

The next day, Coach Gillum pulled Bill aside. "The coaches and I have talked," he said, "and we want more of your energy. What do you say to joining up with the Bananas for the season?"

Soon, one season turned into two, then three, then four, and then a fifth as a professional and part of the Bananas' front office. During that time, he's been one of the most important pieces of our culture.

When we (in)famously introduced kilts as a variant uniform, we went to him to lead the charge. He ended up with a walk-off to win the game.

On the field, he's played every position in the game. Once, during the last home game of the shortened 2020 season, he played every position in *one* game (more on this later).

In another game, at the urging of Kyle Luigs, he made eight switches—batting righty, lefty, righty, etc. during a single at bat. He switched hands for every pitch. Then he drove a base hit up the middle.

Finally, Bill also starred in a ten-part documentary series called *Behind the Mask*, covering his 2020 season during COVID-19.

Bill has become an iconic character, and not just locally in Savannah. Barstool Sports called him the future face of baseball. ESPN features him more than some major leaguers—most prominently, when he introduced himself coming up to bat and when he called his own play *before* it happened. I've seen kids in Kansas City come up to him, starstruck, asking if he's really *the* Bill LeRoy.

Bill played four years on our CPL team, capping it off with one last championship. And now, he has a full-time contract with our professional team and is part of the Bananas' front office.

Look what happened. A player hired for one day became the MVP for four years because he went all-in on Fans First, never missing a chance to engage deeply—with the game, his teammates, and the fans.

You never know how much an effort to entertain could impact someone. It could be something you've done hundreds of times.

It could be something done on a lark, but to that one person experiencing it, it could mean everything. That's what engaging deeply is all about.

But engaging isn't just something you do. It's something you believe. It's something you *feel*. It's something you get fanatical about. It's something you devote yourself to over a whole career. Otherwise, the very idea of trying to make every fan's night special would be exhausting. Here's what we do to foster a culture of connection with the Bananas.

Serve Over Sell

"In most businesses, you think: what is our revenue? What are our expenses? Fans First is an inverse in thinking. We are constantly figuring out what the best possible experience for our fans looks like. How are we rooting out frustration points and friction? How are we providing a remarkable experience for them?"

—JARED ORTON, BANANAS PRESIDENT

Everyone talks about sales and selling and the revenue you get from sales and selling. Why not talk about serving instead? It's a different conversation. It's more inspiring, and in our experience, it brings in more money.

A culture of service starts with the language you use—and the language you don't.

Our language reflects a culture of engagement. We know that people don't want to be sold to. They want to be served. That's why we've eliminated the word *sales* from our vocabulary. That's also why we don't have a Director of Ticket Sales; we have a Director of Tickets. We also have a Ticket Experience Coordinator.

Finance Director Matt Powell was our Ticket Experience Coordinator once upon a time. He came from a background in finance and accounting but started working on the front line with the fans. He's not typical by any means—definitely bananas, but perfect for us.

One day, Matt decided to run a new experiment: he was going to take a different Bananas Member (what we call our season ticket holders) out to lunch every Friday.

Now, inviting total strangers out to lunch is not something that most twenty-three-year-olds are comfortable with. But Matt was committed. Every Friday, he posted on Facebook to members, asking who wanted to go to lunch with him. The first person to respond got a free meal—as well as his undivided attention. Over the next hour or so, Matt learned what these members liked, what they didn't, and what they thought we could do better. (Yep, service is another way to eliminate friction.)

During the height of the COVID-19 pandemic, Matt couldn't take any members out to lunch for a while, but he still found ways to serve. One day, a member posted to Facebook that she'd give anything for Oreo cookies and milk. Without telling anyone, Matt went out, picked up some Oreos and milk, delivered them, and then replied to her post, "Check your mailbox." The fan just about lost her mind.

That's what service over selling is all about.

Flip the Switch

> *"We know we cannot hit a home run with the bases loaded every time we go to the plate. We also know the only way we can get to first base is by going to bat and continuing to swing."*
>
> —WALT DISNEY

"Hey, Jesse, can I talk to you for a minute?"

"Sure, Berry," I said. "What's up?"

That's Berry Aldridge, our Baseball Operations Coordinator. At the time, though, he was a pretty new intern—and he'd just seen me do something he didn't like.

"Your body language toward that fan was not Fans First," he said. "You weren't looking at them head-on, and you didn't connect with them."

Harsh. But he was spot-on. All that fan had wanted was a chance to connect with me, and I'd barely given them the time of day. Instead, I should have flipped the switch and given that fan my full attention.

According to Bananas Coach Tyler Gillum, there are two aspects to being a good Banana: playing good baseball and entertaining. Whichever one you're doing at one time, you should be all-in. Then you can switch to the other. This is a concept that applies not only to our players but to all our interns and staff as well.

Admittedly, I struggle with this. Engaging one-to-one isn't always my strength. I know I need to live in the moment, to give love, and to be present, but my mind is always pulling me toward the next big thing.

To balance this push and pull, I lean on team members like Berry to call me out and help me get better. People like Berry, Emily, Marie, our President Jared, and most of our team are exceptionally good at flipping the switch. Even during the offseason, they take time out of their workday to give fans a tour of the stadium or walk them through the merch store. They ask the fans questions, find out where they're from, and make them feel special.

Following their lead, I've learned to make flipping the switch part of my daily script. These days, sitting with a fan during a game and taking a moment to connect with them on a personal level isn't just a good thing to do. It's what I'm *supposed* to do. Now that I understand that, I couldn't imagine a better way to spend my time.

Listen Carefully. Respond Creatively

"There's something to be said for slowing things down a little bit."

—DARREN ROSS, COO OF MAGIC CASTLE HOTEL

At Magic Castle Hotel, COO Darren Ross trains his staff to "Listen carefully. Respond creatively."

Darren told me the story of a couple that came to the Magic Castle Hotel. The receptionist asked, "What brings you to Hollywood?"

The couple said, "To see Marilyn Monroe." As ginormous Marilyn Monroe fans, they wanted to see her at the wax museum and her star on the Hollywood Walk of Fame.

After they left the room for the day, the receptionist went and bought a Marilyn Monroe poster and put it in their room, writing the caption, "Thanks for coming to see me. Love, Marilyn."

A little creepy in my book, but boy, it made a lasting impression.

A small thing means a lot when it comes to making memories.

Darren's philosophy of listening carefully and responding creatively is part of his bigger focus on stories. As Darren puts it, "Sales aren't contagious. Stories are."

They sure are. From a human standpoint, stories are both fun to make and fun to tell. They make us feel good. From a business standpoint, stories that make us feel good get told and told again. Fans pass their experiences along to future fans, who then have the opportunity to create stories of their own.

That's why, instead of incentivizing his staff on sales or other money-related metrics, he incentivizes them around creating the best stories for their guests. "I want the story," Darren says to his staff, "so make it great."

At the Bananas, we call these stories Fans First Moments. During the season, Jared and I challenge them with a question: "What are the Fans First Moments we're creating tonight?" Is every single fan going to walk home with a story? Maybe not, but that won't stop us from trying to delight and create as many stories as we can.

Stories and moments lay the foundation for who we are and what we stand for. They give us proof that the practice of Fans First works.

Create Your Own Storybook

Most companies have core values, but do they have the stories to back those up? A couple of years after we started, Marie started compiling a storybook of all the Fans First stories that happened during the year. It's helped us with how we onboard new teammates and coach our people. We've learned that stories empower and inspire action more than anything else.

What are your fan stories? Are they compelling? How are you encouraging your team every day to create them? How are you recording them so you can inspire and appreciate your team?

MAKE IT ABOUT THE THREE MS

"Get closer than ever to your customers. So close that you tell them what they need well before they realize it themselves."

—STEVE JOBS

John DiJulius, the author of *Customer Service Revolution*, believes we are entering what he calls the "relationship economy." In this relationship economy, the businesses that connect with fans and build strong relationships will come out on top.

That's why he teaches his staff the FORD concept to build connections with customers. With every customer, team members should ask about their family, occupation, recreation, and dreams.

This is a great concept, and it gels with some of the ideas we've already talked about. The more you pay attention to your fans, the more you listen, ask questions, and act on that information, the more you engage with them and help to create an extraordinary experience.

Nothing matters more than making people feel like they matter.

Our version of the FORD model is what we call the Three Ms: moment, matter, meaning. And nothing exemplifies the three Ms more than Mr. Willie's story.

The story of Mr. Willie is actually one that fans helped make. They're the ones who first introduced us to Mr. Willie when we moved into Grayson Stadium in 2016. In hearing his story, we learned another valuable lesson: if you become known for engaging deeply with fans, for making their moments matter, then your fans will trust you with the stories *they* want told. And as Mr. Willie's story shows, sometimes these stories are *epic*.

Mr. Willie first fell in love with baseball in the 1940s when his father started taking him out to ballgames. Back then, Grayson Stadium—like most of America—was still segregated, but that didn't hamper his interest a bit. By the time he was in high school, Grayson had become desegregated, and Willie had his pick of any seat in the house. Eventually, he settled on his favorite spot high in the grandstands—which remained his seat for years.

In the decades that followed, Savannah baseball fans could count on Mr. Willie to lead the cheer. He was always engaged and yelling during every play. He was always the loudest singer during the seventh-inning (or in our case, second-inning) stretch. He was always happy to yell, "Take a seat!" to visiting players when they struck out.

When the Bananas came to town, he didn't know what to make of us at first. As he put it, "I didn't think people would take to college players." But once he saw what we were all about, he renewed his status as Grayson Stadium's longest-tenured fan.

In 2018, Mr. Willie started missing some games due to health issues. The fans noticed. During the games he was able to make, they would ask him where he'd been and tell him they missed him. This affection has always run both ways. "It's the people next to me who make the ballgame," he says.

As we learned, one reason he was missing games was that couldn't walk like he used to, and his favorite seat had become inaccessible due to the number of stairs he had to walk. We weren't going to let that be the end of the story. If Mr. Willie wanted to come to a game, then Mr. Willie would always have a seat. So, with his permission, we offered him a new seat with fewer stairs. It has a nameplate and everything that says "Mr. Willie."

Before the 2019 season, Mr. Willie's health worsened. We met with him before the season, but he wasn't sure if he was going to make it out. We told him that we knew he'd be strong enough to be there opening night. When he arrived, two of our teammates walked him up to his new seat. When the fans nearby saw him arrive, they stood to cheer him on. Then we announced over the PA, "Mr. Willie is here!" The whole stadium gave him a standing ovation.

In 2021, Mr. Willie was once again back at the ballpark. He's seen every single team Grayson Stadium has hosted—starting with the Indians that played in a brand-new ballpark from 1926 to 1965. But more recently, Mr. Willie could no longer make it up the stairs at all. So we gave him another seat—front row, right behind home plate. As a kid, he couldn't even sit in the grandstands. Now, in his ninth decade as a Savannah baseball fan, he had the best seat in the house. Once again, we introduced Mr. Willie to the packed stadium to open the game. He stood up and yelled, "Play ball!"

The crowd erupted.

Take a seat, Mr. Willie. It's yours whenever you want it.

Be a Moment Maker

What can you notice by watching your customers? Are they wearing merchandise from a certain team? Are they reading a certain book? Are they drinking the same drink every day? What music are they listening to?

To be a Moment Maker, it's simple: People just want to be seen and heard.

Put yourself in fans' shoes and follow these three simple steps: listen carefully, pay attention, and take action.

SHOW UP FOR THE FANS

"For every laugh, there should be a tear."

—WALT DISNEY

Another concept Coach Gillum is big on is what he calls H3, with the Hs standing for hug, high-five, or handshake. "What makes people feel good is connection," Gillum believes, and science backs him up. Studies have shown that being near each other—whether taking a selfie or sharing a hug—makes us feel more connected.

Bananas players learn about the power of H3 on the first day of their orientation—and then they hear it again and again and again. For historically shy players like Kyle Luigs, H3 has given him a script to fall back on so he always knows what to do around the fans. "You have this blueprint that Coach Gillum hammered into our heads," he says. "If you don't know what to do or say, you can give a high-five to a little kid, or you can give a handshake to an old man or a hug to a mom."

H3 is in play from the moment the first fan enters the ballpark. Players are out on the concourse, handing out programs, media guides, and rosters and talking and dancing with the fans. Coach Gillum says. "As soon as you walk into the ballpark, you get to meet a player. For a little kid, that's a life-changing experience."

That experience goes both ways. According to Gillum, the H3 mindset gives the players a sense of who they're actually playing for. It motivates them, gets them excited. The audience is no longer faceless and nameless. The players know these people, and they want to do right by them.

And do right they do. Here are just a few ways the Bananas and our players have taken H3 to a whole new level.

Join the Team

"I feel like I'm on a whole other planet or something because it's the Savannah Bananas. I always thought it would just be baseball, but it's way more than that. It just makes me happier to a whole 'nother level."

—COLTON, BANANAS HIGH-FIVER

Six-year-old Colton is the King Midas of high-fiving. Every hand he touches turns to gold.

Okay, not literally. That would be a disaster. But I've never seen a face that didn't instantly light up like gold when Colton's hand made contact with theirs. It's worked for Will Smith. It's worked for Al Roker. And it's worked for countless other Savannah Bananas fans. This dude just knows how to high-five.

Rewind. It was February of 2019, and Jared and I were attending the Social Media Marketing World Conference in San Diego.

The largest social media marketing conference in the world is quite the event. Over 5,000 people go all-out in creating remarkable and shareable experiences, from live bands to full-on theatrical performances.

But on that first day, taking the escalator up to the main event space, I saw a young man with a sign that really stood out: Free High Fives. I laughed and then immediately went over and gave him my most energetic high-five.

I then wrote in my notebook, "Hire a professional high-fiver for Bananas games."

We left the conference and posted on our social media that we were looking for a professional high-fiver. I thought it was a great gig; you'd get paid to high five people. We even had auditions. No one showed up.

The day before opening day, a mom and a six-year-old came into our office. The kid started high-fiving every person on our team.

I looked at him and said, "You got the job."

The next night he showed up, and we had a jersey printed with the "name" High and number five.

He had one job: to high-five as many fans as possible during a game. That first night he showed up, his mom attached banana-scented hand sanitizer to his belt, and he was ready to go.

He was an instant hit, racking up seventeen to eighteen hundred high fives per game, even though he needed a lot more snack breaks for candy and soda than we'd expected. Well, all in a hard day's work...

Now, even as Colton's gotten older, you can still see him running up and down the concourse high-fiving or air-fiving (COVID-19 made things weird) anyone within arm's reach.

"Don't think about how many people or how many high-fives you get," Colton says. "It's about making people have fun and just you having fun too."

The fun and the fame are nice, Colton admits. But more important is the feeling of family Colton and his mom Krystina have found. "We call it our Banana Fam," Krystina says. "The fans, the staff, the players—it's like a huge family and support system." When Colton's father passed away in 2020, that support system was more important than ever. "I feel like he has big brothers," Krystina says.

No big brother on the Bananas more than Jordan Merrit, Colton's favorite player. So when we auctioned off Jordan's jersey during a promotion, his mother put in a bid. She lost. And Colton was devastated.

To Jordan, that was unacceptable. The second he found out what had happened, he walked into our office and said, "I want to buy an extra jersey and give it to Colton." At the very next game, he held up the jersey for Colton, who ditched his usual high-fivin' style to give Jordan the biggest, hardest hug you'll ever see.

Make Your Fans the Stars

"Children want the same things we want. To laugh, to be challenged, to be entertained and delighted."

—DR. SEUSS

When Bryan Encarnacion, as a sophomore, came for our hometown tryouts, he was impressive. He was the best player, absolutely amazing. Fielding, batting, you name it. But none of those skills shined as bright as his personality.

In the spirit of creating moments, we also let kids participate in the tryouts. Afterward, one starstruck kid asked for Bryan's autograph.

"No," Bryan said. Then he smiled. "Not unless I can have your autograph first."

The boy's face lit up as Bryan took off his Bananas hat and let the boy sign it.

By the end of the season, Bryan's hat was covered with signatures from kids—each a record of his kindness and selflessness toward his biggest fans. Soon other players were following Bryan's lead. These days, check out some of the players' hats, and you'll see them filled front to back with kids' names.

Kyle Luigs exchanged mementos and toys with kids—a bracelet, a squishy ball, a baseball card of Coach Riley (who you'll meet later). Both his locker and road bag were stocked with these little toys—not to mention the bag of all the mementos he'd collected from his fans as part of the swap.

Mike Williams spent an entire season collecting signatures on the sleeve of his jersey, some from kids who didn't even know how to write yet. Mike's idea became so popular with the team that Coach Gillum began making long white sleeves available to every player as part of their uniform.

The players made the *kids* the stars—part of the team. Coach Gillum has even heard kids bragging about which players they'd given autographs to. Not which autographs they'd *received* but which autographs they'd *given*.

As Kyle Luigs puts it, these moments are everything a player could want—and they mean more than he ever would have expected. If you put any kind of effort into entertaining and engaging—whether asking for an autograph or putting a little extra sass into your dance moves, fans will reward you with their love and support all season long.

Making your fans the stars costs next to nothing, but the rewards are infinite. Imagine what your business would look like if you looked for ways to excite kids when they visited. You could offer them souvenirs or take them on tours of the facilities—anything to make them feel appreciated and excited to tell their story.

One Fan at a Time

If you're an entrepreneur or running a business, you may only think of making the biggest impact. You might not think of how to create an impact one person at a time.

If you struggle in this area, you can reflect upon these ideas in your business design:

Does it balance creating the next moment and being present in the current one?

As a leader, how often do you personally engage with your fans? Do you just make big decisions and give orders, or do you also answer the phones?

What's your body language during interactions? Do you face the person? Make eye contact?

The more you engage, the easier and more natural it will become.

THE RULES OF ENGAGEMENT

"There is great comfort and inspiration in the feeling of close human relationships and its bearing on our mutual fortunes—a powerful force, to overcome the 'tough breaks' which are certain to come to most of us from time to time."

—WALT DISNEY

Before we move ahead to the last of our Five Es, I'm going to leave you with one more story.

It was ten thirty at night, about an hour after one of the last games of the season ended. Everyone, even the maintenance crew, had gone home. A little girl stood alone with her father by the gate near first base. She wanted so badly to run the bases.

Bill LeRoy noticed them as he was headed back to the clubhouse. He had just caught an entire game. He was tired, hungry, and sweating like crazy. Still, he saw the father and daughter, and he invited her onto the field and asked if he could run with her. Permission granted, he took her excited little hand, and they took off.

She didn't just want to run the bases once, or twice, or even three times.

She ran them for a full half hour.

And Bill ran with her. Cheering her on.

As Bill rounded the bases for the umpteenth time, he reflected on his first season with the Bananas—a season that almost wasn't.

Bill wasn't even supposed to be a Banana. He was just to come for the opening night, put on a uniform, and watch the game from the dugout before heading back to his hometown for the summer. But the universe aligned to allow him to stay, and he was determined to take advantage of every opportunity.

That's why he stayed to run the bases with that girl—and why he stayed on with the Bananas as a player for three more seasons. In that moment, Bill understood that the goal wasn't to make fans feel like they were on the outside looking in but that they were part of the show too. He was just a normal guy out there having fun, just like them. And maybe, just maybe, one day they'll be down there on the field in his place.

At its heart, engaging deeply is about people. It's about building relationships, not leads. It's about making stories, not sales. It's about appreciating a special group or appreciating that one person is special.

It's about separating the single banana from the bunch and lovingly dousing it in ice cream, hot fudge, and sprinkles and placing a candied cherry on top.

To do this, you observe, listen, and ask questions. You find out what matters to the people standing in front of you. Then, you create a moment that they'll remember forever.

Do for one what you wish you could do for many, and the one will tell the many what you did.

The Bananas Bookshelf

Humanocracy: Creating Organizations as Amazing as the People Inside Them by Gary Hamel and Michael Zanini

Customer Service Revolution by John DiJulius III

EMPOWER ACTION

"I'm not telling you it's going to be easy. I'm telling you it's going to be worth it."

—ART WILLIAMS

It was the first ever grandma beauty pageant. Check that. Great-grandma beauty pageant. In a few minutes, we'd trot out a group of seventy-to-eighty-year-old volunteers—gray-haired women bent with age but bright-eyed and ready to show us how it was done.

If they ever got here.

We were having trouble getting our elderly fans to sign up for this bit. So I called a local retirement home and asked them if they were interested. They were, and they agreed to send a bus over, filled with their finest old ladies.

Finally, the bus arrived five minutes before showtime. The prosaic pageant princesses shuffled out of the bus. I was doing everything I could to speed them up, but there was no rushing these vintage beauties. They shuffled out on their own time.

They'd earned their leisure.

Finally, we were out on the field, and one particular grannie started to separate from the pack. Her name was Gertrude. She was eighty-seven. And she was enjoying her moment in the spotlight.

I went from grannie to grannie, introducing them and asking them questions. When I got to Gertrude, I asked, "If you were on the cover of one magazine, which would it be?"

"*Playboy*, of course!"

The crowd lost it.

But we weren't done. Time for them to strut their stuff.

All the ladies did the same kind of smile, shuffle, and ladylike wave. But not Gertrude. She went for broke and started dancing—slowly rotating her lower half, complete with hip thrusts. Twice.

Gertrude was a star. And the hands-down winner.

"We never do this at the nursing home," she cackled at me as she ambled off the field.

"Of course you don't, Gertrude," I said, giving her a big hug.

A shame, really, that nursing homes don't have more...pageants.

Gertrude went out in front of a crowd of thousands. She danced. She had fun. And she didn't give two flying bananas what people thought of her or her antics.

If a little old lady can show this much courage, so can you.

All you have to do is get off that bus, grab your walker if you need to, and take that first, feeble step. If you're uncomfortable, even better. Austin the Awkward Rapper was uncomfortable, too, and things couldn't have turned out better for him.

Too many people are too scared to be uncomfortable. It takes courage to put yourself out there, so they just stick with the status quo instead.

Your job as a leader is to give your team a little push when they need it. Or entrance music. Everybody likes entrance music.

That's why our fifth and final E is Empower Action. The greatest accomplishments, the greatest achievements, the greatest things that you'll ever do in life often come from doing things you've never done before. But sometimes, it takes a little encouragement and empowerment to do it.

SWING HARD IN CASE YOU HIT IT

"Swing hard in case you hit it."

—KERRY COLE, MY DAD

I was five years old when I first played baseball with a team. It was the rookie league at the South Shore Baseball Club in Hingham, Massachusetts.

My first time up to bat, I was visibly nervous. I slowly walked up to the plate, afraid to hit in front of everybody.

My dad, seeing my struggle from the sidelines, yelled out to me, "Hey, Jess, swing hard...in case you hit it!"

It was a pivotal moment in my young life, and his words have stayed with me ever since. As I progressed in my baseball career, I certainly swung and missed a lot, but when I made contact, I hit the ball very hard.

The person who had the most hits in major league baseball history was not Babe Ruth. (Sorry, Babe. You can't have all the glory.) It was Pete Rose. He had over 4,000 hits. He also had over 14,000 at-bats. He had 2,000 more at-bats than anyone else who played the game. Of course, he had more hits. He just kept coming to bat.

He also made nearly 10,000 outs in his career. But we don't remember those. We remember his hits.

My dad always reminded me of this when I was learning to play baseball. Sure, I swung and missed a ton. But so did Pete Rose. As we saw in "Experiment Constantly," so did Reggie Jackson. And they're all-time greats.

It's not what you miss; it's what you hit in life. That's what you'll remember. That's what everyone will remember. That's why, whenever he saw me up at the plate acting like I was unsure of myself, he would say to me later, "Jesse, swing hard in case you hit it." He knew I was going to miss—a lot. But he wanted me to miss the right way: focused on the best possible results.

You're going to swing and miss. It's okay.

Your team is going to swing and miss. That's okay too.

As long as you're swinging in service to your team and your fans, you're growing in the right direction.

If you want to empower action in your team, start by changing the mindset of your organization. Instead of focusing on failure, focus on what you're trying to do. What new chances are you going to take? What new things are you going to do? Will these new things make you feel uncomfortable? Scared?

I hope so. If you're not scared a little, you're not thinking big enough. That's empowerment: the will to step up to bat even when you're scared—and to keep stepping up no matter what happens.

EMPOWER YOUR TEAM

"Great leaders are willing to let go of control for the growth of their people and their fans. The greatest leaders make the least amount of decisions."

—REED HASTINGS

It's hard to have the courage to do things differently if you live and work in an environment where you're constantly afraid of failure.

Too many businesses operate within a punishment system. When something doesn't go well, the powers that be find someone to blame. The result? No more innovation. No more risk-taking. It's just not worth it if something goes wrong.

The Bananas have flipped that mindset on its head. Instead of a punishment system, we have a rewards system. We encourage our team to try things that may not work (remember: experiment constantly), and we celebrate the outcome no matter what. We celebrate the big wins and the tiny victories. We even celebrate the failures for the chance they gave us to learn something new.

Here's what that culture of empowerment looks like in action.

Butt In

"Never take yourself too seriously. You might just bring joy to people's lives."

—PATRICK BRIODY, BANANAS WORLD TOUR DIRECTOR

For years, Carson Bowen had a string of titles and successes across the Coastal Plain League. He thrilled fans in the broadcast booth. He boosted attendance in Wilmington by 450 percent in just two seasons.

He was overqualified for the role of ticket experience coordinator that we offered him—almost comically so. Still, he was happy to take the pay cut and come down to Savannah.

Why? Because where there were Bananas, there was also opportunity. As Carson puts it, our initial pitch to have him come to Savannah to run and refine our existing system wasn't especially exciting. But as he says, "There's a non-zero chance that the Bananas will be playing baseball on the dadgum moon by 2030." And that *is* exciting.

Carson knew he'd made the right choice when he suggested we put buttcheeks—yes, you read that correctly—on our tickets and he wasn't immediately shot down. Why buttcheeks? Because "a Banana with butt cheeks is objectively hilarious." Now Carson gets to brag that "we're the first sports team to ever put buttcheeks on tickets."

So what made Carson confident he could make such a cheeky suggestion? Fans First. "From Day One (or even before), I knew what I should be doing and how I should be acting," Carson says. "It's a simple mantra, but it's freeing to have a North Star like that. I knew I could be myself. I knew I could be goofy and was given sweeping permission to inject fun and silliness into phone calls and emails, and I was empowered to help people feel good."

At the Bananas, we celebrate every idea that our team brings to the table—no ifs, ands, or butts.

Listen and Act (or Care?)

"As a mama, you always hope your kids are safe and loved. This gift of family at a time when we really needed it will never, ever be forgotten in ours. She'll be back at the stadium running from patio to patio, tending bar, feeding players, slinging merch, and having an absolute blast soon. If you see her, hug her for her mama. Thank you to the entire organization for loving your people well. I'm so glad my kid gets to be one of them!"

—JENNIFER WHITE, PROUD MOTHER OF A BANANAS INTERN

Fans First Director Marie Matzinger has been with the Bananas since first joining us right out of college in 2015. Not only does she feel an acute sense of ownership for our culture, but she also remembers what it can feel like when you're just starting out.

Every night after a show, we have a postgame debriefing where we talk through the night, celebrate any particularly fun Fans First moments, and talk about what we could do better for the next game. One night in 2021, after our postgame chat, she called everyone to the Stadium Club. Once everyone was in the room, she led everyone over to the TV and turned it on.

On the screen was the family of one of our interns. They looked at the camera and gave a brief speech. "We miss you. We're proud of you. We know you're making a real impact. We can't wait to have you home, and we love you!"

The video switched to another intern's family with a similar message of support and love. Then another. Then another. And so on down the line.

There wasn't a dry eye in the place.

This is true caring. A gift. Marie saw that some of our interns were experiencing some midseason homesickness, and she decided to create this moment for them to help make them feel a little better. And how much did this cost us? Other than a little bit of Marie's time, nothing. She saw a need and acted. And it meant so much.

Being Fans First means taking care of your First Fans: your team. All our success in Bananaland depends on the culture we've created with our team. It's not just about creating the moments; it's caring about what moments you create.

EMPOWER YOURSELF

"What do you think?"

—KEN SILVER

A man named Ken Silver gave me my first job as the general manager of his team when I was just twenty-three years old. He was one of my first mentors and gave me my first big opportunity.

That first year as GM, I pitched him an idea. It was a game that started at midnight on a Friday night. A second-shift game. It would be billed as a huge late-night festival. What were his thoughts on it?

But he would never give me his thoughts. He would just say, "Jesse, what do you think?"

And I'd go off. "I'm thinking about doing a grandma beauty pageant. I'm thinking about doing FlatulenceFun Nights. I'm thinking about doing Mighty Dollar Mondays with one-dollar specials." I pitched him hundreds of ideas.

And he always said, "What do you think?"

Eventually, I caught on to what he was doing. I was the general manager. I was in charge of this team. It wasn't what he thought. It was what *I* thought. Instead of coming to him, I asked myself first, "What do you think?" Then, I took ownership, made the decision, and told Ken what we were doing.

If you want your team to function without you, you have to embody that question whenever your team seeks approval for their ideas. What do you think?

It's the best question to ask—and one that I've carried forward as a leader.

When Zack, our Director of Entertainment, joined up with the Bananas, he and I began doing laps around the field to talk over the show and compare our notes. What promotions did we like? What should we do differently? What new things could we do in the next game?

About twenty games in, a funny thing happened: our notes were perfectly aligned. He saw the same opportunities for improvement that I did—but with his own spin that always takes things to the next level. He's been empowered to think on his own, to see what's best for our fans.

As a result, he doesn't need to run his ideas by me anymore. He knows what he would do, and the fans are in better hands for it.

Here are a couple of other examples of what it means to empower a team of leaders committed to thinking for themselves and making a difference.

Take the Walk

"It's the words we use when we talk to them. The way that we treat them from the second they pull up to our parking penguins to the second they hang out at our Party in the Plaza. It's heartwarming knowing that we're a company that really cares so much about the people who come in and the people who leave. We want them to come back. It's right there: Fans First. I've learned so many things just from that."

—JOHNATHAN WALTERS, BANANAS STADIUM
OPERATIONS COORDINATOR

It's the end of a game and people are going home. It's pouring. Like, biblically pouring. That happens in the South: sometimes the sky just opens up and dumps buckets without warning.

Since our first rain delay, we've learned a few things. We line up our staff with umbrellas, and they take turns walking fans to their cars in the parking lot. They always hold the umbrella directly over the fans, getting wet in the process. Then, it's a race back to the gate to pick up another fan.

Laura, an intern just two weeks in, is approached by an older gentleman, and they amble away. After thirty minutes, I suddenly realize she's still gone and think, *Whoa, where is she?* Just as I'm about to rally the troops, Laura walks up.

She's drenched.

"Where have you been?" I ask, grateful she's okay (if a little wet).

"I walked a guy all the way home to his doorstep," Laura says. "He told me he lived right down the road and had walked to the game." As it turned out, "right down the road" translated to *a mile* down the road. Suffice to say, Laura got her steps in for that day.

I'm speechless, which is rare for me. Then Laura looks up at me. "Fans first, right?"

Right. Now *that's* going the extra mile to keep Fans First.

You Can Make a Difference

"Grayson Stadium and Savannah baseball has been a fixture in Savannah forever. It has endured many changes through the years. As a Savannah girl born and raised here, Grayson Stadium holds a lot of memories for me. Now I have the opportunity to share this legacy with my grandchildren, my future. Lives are touched and changed. Memories and traditions are made. Families bond together. Couples enjoy a date night. Church groups attend. Teenagers and their friends have a place to go, and businesses engage in camaraderie. Kids watch the players and dream. They dream of becoming baseball stars! It is a beacon of good, clean, fun entertainment for all."

—LISA J. ROBERTSON, BANANAS FAN

Back in 2016, when Berry Aldridge was still just an intern and making thank-you calls to ticket purchasers, he was having trouble reaching a family, the Nunn family, who had bought eight tickets to the show. Finally, Berry got in touch with the father. He learned that the wife and mother had bought tickets for their seven kids to go to a game—and then she had tragically died.

Shocked and speechless, Berry managed to get out, "I'm so sorry to hear that," before ending the conversation.

Then he walked into my office and told me the story. "What do we do?" he said.

Channeling Ken Silver, I replied, "What do you think?"

"Well, I'd really love to get the kids and dad out here and create something special for them," he said.

I agreed. "What ideas do you have? What would make it special?"

As it turned out, Berry had plenty of ideas—and he was ready to put them into action, planning the whole night for the Nunn family all on his own. When the family arrived on the night of the game, Berry seated them in the front row and had all the players come and deliver autographed bats and balls and hang out with the family for about a half hour before the game. Then Berry presented the dad with a jersey with his wife's name. Its number was the number of years they'd been married.

After the game, Berry and the father were chatting a little more, and the father shared that these Bananas tickets were the last gift his wife had given their kids—and he couldn't have imagined a better gift! Without Berry, the family might never have come to the game. Thanks to Berry's effort, the family was able to make that last gift—that last story of their wife and mother—special.

Imagine what your business would look like if your interns or new hires brought the same level of care and agency to their work—all because they were empowered to think for themselves. What amazing things would you be able to do for your fans?

Sing It for the Back Rows!

Every moment, every touchpoint is a chance to engage and create fans. It's also a chance to find and showcase your team's unique talents.

A few years ago, we asked Nicole Charot, one of our interns and a talented singer and songwriter, if she could write and perform a fun song for the pregame announcements. She rewrote the lyrics of popular songs like "Old Town Road," "No Tears Left to Cry," and "All-Star" to share our concessions and no-smoking policies.

That season, our whole team was singing Nicole's new adaptations of "No Tears Left to Cry:" "Smoking is prohibited inside Grayson Stadium. So please take it outside. There's a place in the front to smoke if you want, so thank you for all your cooperation."

If you embrace and empower your people to use their unique talents, they'll make the ordinary extraordinary.

EMPOWER YOUR FANS

"I know that whatever nerves I have will melt away when I remind myself that we've got a North Star— keep having fun, and fans will have fun. Put Fans First, and good things will happen."

—CARSON BOWEN, BANANAS TICKET EXPERIENCE DIRECTOR

There is a line between thinking of each fan as a person you want to share a moment with and thinking of fans as a thing that looks good on social media. The drive to make a moment should never stem from *your* interest. It stems from *the fan's* interest.

This isn't hard to put into practice. For every decision, start with them. How do you lift them up? How do you make them feel special?

Well, you invite them to co-create your business with you.

I Dare You

"What makes me a fan of the organization is the way we continuously want to move forward and progress. We never want to flatline. We never want to slow down. We always want to keep going. We always want to keep pushing content. We always want to better serve our fans. We always want to make it better than it was the day before."

—JOHNATHAN WALTERS,
BANANAS STADIUM OPERATIONS COORDINATOR

We let our fans pick the team's name. The mascot. The jerseys. We let fans design our merch. And we make that participation mean something.

Our first T-shirt design contest winner, Catherine, got a VIP experience: a staff member shuttled her and her friends to the park. They got a tour of the locker room. They were on the field for the pre-game show. They had their favorite drinks served at their reserved seats. Once again: engage deeply.

But don't forget to experiment too. Over the years, we've become more and more comfortable about letting fan participation literally affect the outcome of the game. Like all experimenting, sometimes these Fans First efforts to empower don't go so well.

Once, we let our fans pick who was going to pitch in the game. They picked a University of Georgia closer—who then gave up six runs. Not exactly the outcome we'd hoped for, and it left Coach Gillum looking like he'd found a bruised banana in his sundae. But we wanted fans to feel like it was their team.

Yes, some opportunities we create don't go how we script them out. But we've learned that more often than not, things work out better when you go Fans First.

Once you make fans, you have to trust them.

In 2021, we took to TikTok to have our fans pick which dares our players would do during a game. They had plenty of great ideas to choose from:

- Act like there's a bee chasing you in the outfield.

- Dive on a routine fly ball.

- Play "Chubby Bunny" in the middle of a game with Big League Chew.

- Let the boys give you a haircut before the game.

- Do high knees while you're in the field.

- Sit crisscross applesauce and play with the grass like an eight-year-old during the game.

- Bat with a banana in your back pocket

Hundreds of people respond to these dare posts, chiming in on what they think we should do during games. And then we actually do it.

That's where the magic happens. The more we demonstrate that we're willing to play *with* them rather than just in front of them, the more empowered they feel to go bananas with us.

Give and You Shall Receive

"There's not really a more loyal fanbase than Savannah. It's a two-way street. If you're invested in the fans and doing Fans First—whether it's someone's first game or sixtieth—you're going to get that return a hundredfold."

—KYLE LUIGS, BANANAS PITCHER

Biko Skalla is the Bananas' master broadcaster. He calls all the games, including away ones. But here was Biko's problem: the Coastal Plain League gives home teams exclusive video rights, which means that when we're on the road, we can't broadcast any footage of the game on the field.

Sure, we could still do audio-only broadcasts at these games, but Biko felt they didn't add enough value for our fans. Luckily, Biko, with the help of Jared, had another idea: he could draw everything that happened on a big whiteboard. The camera would be trained on him and his whiteboard, and he would draw pitchers, batters, and baserunners, scribbling wildly all over the field when a ball was put in play.

The fans loved these goofy whiteboard broadcasts. What they didn't love, however, was Biko's dried-out markers. He needed an upgrade—and fast.

The fans leaped to the rescue. Dani Lynn Dispaltro sent a brand-new four-pack of markers, and then Bob Swisher sent in an extender pack of markers with a bunch of new colors to spice up the broadcast.

Just like that, Biko's whiteboard game had been taken to another level. But still, to anyone watching, it was obvious Biko was juggling a lot of moving pieces between calling the game, managing his scorebook, drawing on the whiteboard, and posting Facebook comments. He needed help.

Enter Lori Flippin Bode. An enthusiastic aunt of one of our players, Lori made little magnets for all thirty-eight players on the roster, as well as an assortment of magnets for balls, strikes, outs, pitchers, and hitters. She even created magnets for the Bacon and the Blowfish, our biggest rivals.

Not only was Biko blown away when he received the magnets in the mail, but he was able to stay on top of his many tasks much, much better. How's that for getting your fans in the game?

FANS EMPOWER YOU

"I dream, I test my dreams against my beliefs, I dare to take risks, and I execute my vision to make those dreams come true."

—WALT DISNEY

So what does all this fan empowerment do?

We have over ten thousand people on a waitlist for tickets. If a game gets added to the schedule, it sells out within hours. Our merchandise is sold all over the world and accounts for millions of dollars in revenue each year.

We never tell our fans to buy tickets or merch. We spend zero marketing dollars on selling gear because we know that people don't like being sold to.

Still, the Bananas brand has continued to grow beyond us—and beyond anything we could have dreamed.

This is the fans' team now. They help make its decisions. They help improve the show. They share in our joys, disappointments, and challenges.

Our fans wear their Bananas gear to feel that sense of belonging and ownership over the brand they helped create. They're proud to be a part of the show, and they want to tell the world.

During the height of the COVID-19 pandemic in 2020, we struggled with the decision of whether to play that season. We lost sleep over it. We had to decide between safety and giving the fans the entertainment they so much wanted and needed. When we were cleared to play and ultimately decided to go forward, we had to make sure it was safe for our fans to come back.

To start, that meant playing at 25 percent capacity. It was a huge hit for us financially, but the decision was still a no-brainer: Fans First, Entertain Always—and always means always.

We just hoped they would show up.

They did. And once the ballgames were back underway, we got to hear their stories.

Like the family who drove forty hours from Utah to come to a game.

Like the season ticket holder who told us, tears streaming down his face, that he'd been in a dark place, but knowing we were going to play, and finally coming out to a game, had saved his life. Finally, he could feel normal again—sing and dance again. He had hope.

Even when faced with a difficult decision during a pandemic, the fans guided us. We knew what the fans needed, and their response proved to us that we were right. We made the decision based on our core values.

Let the Fun Grow

"A week or two into the 2020 season, I received a box of twenty-four mechanical pencils from Bananas Assistant Coach Phill Shallenberger. It turned out his wife Courtney had gotten the pencils for me because throughout the first few broadcasts, I kept dropping my pencils on the floor, which I would announce on the broadcast, and then I would have to get off my chair to go retrieve them. Now I could just grab another from the box and pick up all my fallen pencils once the game was over. It was a really nice gesture, and the box kept me stocked on pencils for the rest of the season.

The only problem, it turns out, is I constantly break the tip of mechanical pencils, which turned into another running joke throughout the season. About a month into the year or so, the fans decided they could create a drinking game for broadcasts based on my many quirks and odd terminologies, and drinking every time I broke a pencil tip was one of the first rules they created."

–BIKO SKALLA, BANANAS BROADCAST ENTERTAINER

PAY IT FORWARD

"I'm for the dreamer. The only really important things in history have been started by the dreamers. They never know what can't be done. I have wandered through life on the philosophy that if you wish for something to happen and do everything possible to make it happen and convince yourself that it is going to happen, who knows? It may happen!"

—BILL VEECK

A group of DJs from all over the country met together at a Bananas game. They'd planned the trip out a year in advance and were soaking in the experience. They even got to hear me give a talk about creating Fans First Moments, and they were interested in practicing it themselves.

Enter Christopher, the charming server for their section. The DJs struck up a conversation with him and learned that he was a huge Reba McEntire fan. In fact, his whole family was—and it was their dream to see Reba in concert.

The DJs decided to make that dream a reality. Pooling their money together, twenty dollars a person, they raised over seven hundred dollars by the end of the game. Then, they bought Christopher two tickets—front row, VIP—to a Reba McEntire concert.

When they told him what they'd done, Christopher couldn't contain his tears.

Think about what just happened. Here was a group of Bananas fans. They'd heard about Fans First and creating Fans First Moments, and they decided they wanted to be a part of that magic. Seeing what the Fans First Way was all about, they were empowered to act.

You can create these moments too. More importantly, you can empower others to want to create these moments on their own. You can inspire people to think about others in ways they never would have thought to do.

So what's holding you back? Is it the fear of failure? The fear of judgment? The fear of swinging big and missing?

Remember, people won't remember you for your failures. They'll remember you for your successes. They'll remember that you kept coming to bat. They'll remember you never stood still when you had a chance to act.

The Bananas are living proof. No one remembers our first brutal opening night. Or our failed horse race promotion. Or the halftime bagpipe band that put them to sleep.

They remember us for the moments we created for them. They remember us for how we made them feel. They remember us for inviting them to stand with us and to believe that anything is possible—and that anyone can act.

This can be the mindset at your business too.

Empower action by encouraging your team to feel ownership, by encouraging your fans to give their input, and by encouraging yourself to ask one question: what do you think?

Let go to grow. Both for yourself and for those who support you.

Because you never know when you'll need to call on those superfans.

Okay, that's a wrap on Part 2. You now have all the lowdown on all the Five Es.

It's a lot. You're not going to master them all overnight. Decide which E you want to focus on—eliminating friction, entertaining, experimenting, engaging, or empowering—and spend the next year making that your driving force.

After you get the hang of that E, add in one or two more. And then watch the wins pile up.

The Bananas Bookshelf

No Rules, Rules: Netflix and the Culture of Reinvention by Reed Hastings and Erin Meyer

Know What You're FOR: A Growth Strategy for Work, an Even Better Strategy for Life by Jeff Henderson

Intention Imperative: 3 Essential Changes That Will Make You a Successful Leader Today by Mark Sanborn

Part 3: The Aftershow

CREATE AN UNFORGETTABLE EXPERIENCE

"The price of inaction is far greater than the cost of a mistake."

—MEG WITTMAN, CEO OF EBAY

When your mantra is Fans First, Entertain Always, then you must constantly be on the lookout for elements of your experience that go against that. Sometimes, this means taking a long, hard look at the experience you already have in place—and maybe even blowing it up to make it better.

This is exactly what South Carolina's own Shoreline Construction did. In September of 2018, I was giving a speech on how to go Fans First to a bunch of business owners in Bluffton. In the audience was Chris Dalzell, Shoreline's owner, furiously taking notes from start to finish. When he came up to speak with me afterward, he said one thing was clear: his company needed to change.

Soon after, he called a big team dinner. All of Shoreline's employees were invited to attend, as well as their spouses. Surrounding their table was a series of whiteboards, and in front of each team member's place at the table was a pad of sticky notes. As the evening kicked off, Chris said their goal was to answer four core questions:

- What is our client experience now?

- What do we want it to be?

- How can we be different?

- What is the wildest thing you can think of?

Everyone joined in. No idea was off the table—rap videos, mariachi bands and margaritas at house closings, drone footage, sign spinners, ribbon-cutting ceremonies, you name it. By the end of the evening, they had completely rethought their customer—scratch that, *fan* experience. And just like that, they had taken their first step to completely transforming their company.

I'd love to say that it was happily ever after from that point on, but creating change is messy. Shoreline had a lot of big ideas, but they still had to sharpen up their delivery.

As part of their new experience, Shoreline began including a ribbon-cutting ceremony for all their new homes, complete with a red carpet and champagne. At their first ribbon-cutting ceremony, however, they forgot to put the champagne on ice.

Worse, they left it in one of the trucks. So there they were in the South Carolina summer, toasting their new homeowners with hot champagne.

It wasn't the perfect rollout they were hoping for, but as we've seen, mess-ups and do-overs are part of the process. The hard work of shifting their perspective was behind them. They had looked at the problems in their industry—bad communication, delayed completion dates, cost overruns—and created a plan to do something different.

Instead of asking themselves whether they could squeeze out more revenue, instead of asking how they could grow their digital footprint on social media, instead of wondering how they could cut costs on labor and materials, instead of looking at all those wonderful metrics that traditional businesses cherish, they asked how they could make their fans' experience better.

Fast forward. A couple from New Jersey bought a home from Shoreline Construction. They signed a contract and told the Shoreline team they were coming into town both for a visit and to celebrate their anniversary. Since the couple was still pretty new to the area, they asked the Shoreline team for dining recommendations.

Here, the Shoreline team seized on a golden opportunity. First, one of the team members offered to pick the couple up from the airport and take them to a one-of-a-kind place they knew about.

That one-of-a-kind place? Well, it turned out to be the couple's unfinished house. It didn't have a roof yet. The framing was barely done. But it did have a full dinner spread, complete with twinkle lights and a fully catered anniversary meal. The wife broke out crying and screaming with joy!

It wasn't just that the Shoreline team had created such an unforgettable experience. It was that they came up with the whole idea on their own—with no help from Chris or anyone else in senior leadership.

To me, that's the essence of what it means to create an unforgettable experience. It's never about one person driving it. It's about a team buying into a shared vision and getting fanatical about delivering in every moment and at every touchpoint.

These days, Shoreline Construction doesn't have customers. They have fans. They don't close deals. They have first-day celebrations. By focusing on the people they serve, they saw all the opportunities to make things better—and armed with a powerful new vision, they committed to change.

If you want to stand out, think about what that perfect fan experience is, and do it. That's what part 3 of the book is all about.

GET OFF THE SIDELINES AND GET IN THE DANCE

*"I've got a dream too. It's about singing and dancing
and making people happy. That's the kind of dream
that gets better the more people you share it with."*

—KERMIT THE FROG

Five-year-old Navah can dance. Even if she's wearing an adult-sized Bananas shirt and hat that makes it hard to move. Even if she's wearing a blindfold.

That's why Navah was the winner of our dance-off contest.

As her reward, Navah not only got a crown, but she also got to go on a "date" with long-term Bananas pitcher Kyle Luigs. Over by the Bananas dugout, their own personal bistro table covered with a yellow tablecloth, they enjoyed fried chicken together.

Navah told Kyle this was her very first Bananas game. Kyle suggested that she enjoy her second game as soon as possible and invited her to Thursday night's game so she could watch him pitch.

"I'll have to ask my mommy," she said. Naturally.

To round out the date, Kyle gave her a yellow rose, and then they enjoyed one more dance on top of the dugout. To make sure he was eye-level with her, Kyle danced the whole song on his knees, coaching her through the steps, and ending with a big dip.

It was an incredibly sweet moment. And apparently, a lot of the other fans thought so too. The video got over a million views on Facebook.

That's what creating an unforgettable experience is all about—and how a special moment for one girl can become a heartwarming memory for a legion of fans across the globe.

I've said it time and time again in this book, but I'll say it again: it doesn't matter what business you're in. You can create those moments for your fans too.

You just have to execute.

In just five years, the Bananas were able to resurrect baseball in Savannah, to bring Grayson Stadium back to life in a big way, and to give the community something to be proud of. This was only possible because we had a vision that we loved, and we were willing to break the mold and put every ounce of energy we had into making it happen.

Why? Because we knew that none of this would work any other way.

Here in the last part of the book, I dare you to imagine what you can accomplish in your business over the next five years. I dare you to look at your business and ask how you can take it from unremarkable to unforgettable.

Just remember: this is a lot of work.

So check yourself and check your team. Do you believe in this? Is it rooted in your culture? Are you passionate about going Fans First and creating an unforgettable experience? Are you a fanatic?

You can't force it, and you can't go halfway. Either you're in, or you're out.

Here in part 3, you'll learn how to promote your new Fans First values to yourself, your team, and your fans. Finally, we'll give you a drop of banana-flavored courage to Go Bananas!

Here we go. This is the final push, your moment to run through a brick wall like the Kool-Aid Man. Break through that wall— and then Kool-Aid showers for everyone!

Bananas Bookshelf

The Red-Carpet Way: Extraordinary Experiences that Lift People Up! by Donna Cutting

©MTPhotography

BE YOUR OWN BIGGEST FAN

*"What is the ultimate qualification of success? For
me, it's not how much time you spend doing what
you love. It's how little time you spend doing what
you hate."*

—CASEY NEISTAT

It's the last home game of the 2020 season. And it might be Bill
LeRoy's last game as a Banana.

If he's going to go out, then he's going to go out in glory. Soon,
Bill and teammate Kyle Luigs propose an idea: they should play
every single position during the game.

So that's exactly what they do. But we don't stop there. Might as
well mic Bill up while we're at it. Soon, we've rigged him up. His
AirPods feed into the phone in his back pocket, which is calling
out to the broadcast booth so they can hear everything.

We didn't know if any of this would even work—but we did know
that it would make a great show.

Fast forward a couple of hours. The Bananas have just come back from a four-run deficit, and then a moonshot from Kyle ties it up. At this point, Bill is all amped up. The momentum is on the Bananas' side, and as he trots back out to the field for the ninth inning, he thinks, *It would be a shame if we didn't win this one.*

There's just one problem: Bill's pitching.

He hasn't pitched since seventh grade.

Luckily, Bill only needs one out. As he walks out to the mound, he hears Bon Jovi's "Dead or Alive" come over the speakers. The crowd starts chanting his name. His heart's racing, but he doesn't show it. Instead, he just tips his hat and starts his warm-up tosses.

Fastball. Dead center. *That was a lot better than anything I threw in the bullpen,* he thinks. He tosses a few more—all fire, all strikes.

The batter steps in. Bill's nerves flare up. He's feeling gassed already. Whose bright idea was this?

Bill gets two quick strikes with a couple of fastballs. Then he throws a curve that the batter barely gets a piece of and fouls back. Bill goes back to his fastball, and the batter smokes it to the outfield for a hit. Runner on first.

Bill's heart is in his throat. The crowd around him grows louder, swallowing him up in cheers. Bill digs down and chucks another fastball.

Ground ball, left side. The third baseman makes a diving play and fires a laser to first. Out number three. Game over.

Bill marches off the mound and raises a hand, and the fans find a new level of loud previously unknown to humankind.

This is what it looks like when you're your own biggest fan.

Changing the game, breaking the rules, creating an unforgettable experience—it all starts from the same place: believing in yourself. Players like Bill LeRoy rise to the occasion because what they do gives them passion, purpose, and energy. In those moments, it's not about chasing money. It's about having fun, about feeling connected to everyone around you, about being a part of something bigger than yourself.

But to capture that feeling, you must believe in what you're doing and love the journey. If you want to be the best for your team—and the best for your fans—you need to be the best for yourself.

But don't just take my word for it.

In this chapter, we're going to look at what it's like to be your own biggest fan. And what better way to learn than from some of the biggest fans I know?

DO WHAT YOU LOVE, NOT WHAT YOU HATE

"Have the courage to follow your heart and intuition. They somehow already know what you truly want to become."

—STEVE JOBS

I first met Jake Brewer when he was an intern for our previous team in Gastonia, North Carolina. When I took over as general manager and started changing things up, he wasn't sure what to make of it. To put it bluntly, as a baseball purist, he thought what we were trying to do was nuts. But he was a small-town boy with a big heart, and eventually he bought into the Fans First Way.

After years of working closely with Jake, we went to launch the Savannah Bananas. Jake eventually went to work for a minor league team close to home, but he quickly found something was missing in his new role. Where was the spontaneity, the freedom to be yourself, the eagerness to try new things?

Eventually, Jake decided his time in baseball was done. But if he was going to go out, he was going to go out the Fans First Way. So he called us up and asked if he could retire a Banana. Happy to oblige, we signed him to a one-day contract as the Ticket Leprechaun for our St. Patrick's Day in July game.

Jake was like a fish in water. He threw Lucky Charms into the crowd. He jigged. He even hopped a fence to fix our manual scoreboard in full leprechaun attire. He was the happiest—and tallest—leprechaun you'd ever meet.

Then, after the game, he gave one of the most moving, profound speeches I've ever heard. Here's a part of it:

> This organization gave me a platform to care about people. That's what it's always been about for me. If I can make somebody laugh, smile, create a memory, that's what's important. I never would have thought that I was in the business of making people's lives better. To come here tonight and finish my career at home means so much to me. I just wanted to feel that magic one last time. I may only be Fans First in a contract for one day, but I'll be Fans First in my heart forever.

Above all, being your own biggest fan means following your heart. It means believing in yourself. It means being unafraid of putting yourself out there and having fun. It means giving yourself permission to go absolutely bananas.

But don't take my word for it. Take it from one of the greatest innovators of all time: Steve Jobs.

In his book *The Innovation Secrets of Steve Jobs,* author Carmine Gallo cites "Do what you love" as Jobs's first principle driving his success. As Gallo explains, Jobs fiercely believed that people couldn't come up with creative ideas and innovation if they weren't passionate about what they were doing or who they worked for. "The only thing that kept me going was that I loved what I did," Jobs once said during a Stanford

University commencement speech. "The only way to do great work is to love what you do."

When you love what you do, you feel passionate about what you do. Sometimes that passion is expressed by sharing what you love. Sometimes that passion is expressed by eliminating the things you hate. Remember what we said in the Eliminate Friction chapter: if you want to create raving fans, then stop doing what your fans hate. From there, it's just a matter of turning it into something you love. You need both these drivers to persevere.

This principle doesn't just apply to your business. It applies to each of us as people as well. To eliminate friction from your own life, stop doing the things you hate, and start doing the things you love.

When I put on my yellow tux, I don't become a character. The Yellow Tux Guy is really me—and I love doing it. I'm all-in on being an entertainer, and I'm always looking for new ways to bring the fun.

You don't become a Ticket Leprechaun, a Yellow Tux Guy, or a Steve Jobs unless you've tapped into something inside yourself and fully believe in and love what you're doing. This is true for every member of the Bananas show, from the break-dancing first base coach to the Banana Nanas. Each of our characters is their own entity, makes their own fun contributions, and expresses their own courage—even if that means taking a shot in the nanners, like poor, poor Patrick Briody.

They've bought into the Bananas because they first bought into themselves. They became their own fanatics. And many of them made themselves known to us not through a job call but through their own heartfelt desire to spread their love and spirit. These characters are as diverse as they are lovable. But if there's one thing they have in common, it's energy.

How Would You Retire?

Imagine a scenario like Jake Brewer's. If you could retire from any company, which would it be? Why? What impassioned speech would you give on your last day? Now use that knowledge to instill those passions and values into your own company.

THE BONUS E: ENERGY

"Change your 'have-tos' to 'get-tos.'"

—JON GORDON

How often do you come home exhausted from work, as if all the energy has been drained right out of you? How do you feel about performing the rest of your day? Do you have enough energy to give to your spouse, your kids, or your hobbies?

Probably not. When you're feeling drained, it's hard to muster up the energy even to do the things you love. I know because

I talk to people like this every time I deliver a keynote. Afterward, a few people will always come up to me and say they wish they had my energy. Then they'll ask where it all comes from.

My answer is simple: I do things that give me energy.

So do the Bananas' biggest superfans. Let's see what they do to keep showing up to Grayson every game ready to bring the noise.

Check the Energy Levels

"There's always a story that comes with being recognized as the Banana Beard guy. You know, I like that. That's amazing."

—ADAM "BANANA BEARD" GAZDA

Hateful things zap energy; loving things give it to you. As much as I hate to use the word "audit," I frequently audit my schedule. That way, I can clearly see the things I do that don't give me energy. I delegate as much of that work as I can to the people who are better at it than me and who actually enjoy doing it.

Then, I focus on myself.

I have a morning ritual that works to give me energy. I was first inspired by Hal Elrod's book *Miracle Morning*, where he shares his morning life SAVERS: silence, affirmations, visualization, exercise, reading, and scribing. I follow similar savory habits.

(No, it's not eating a banana.) I read. I run and listen to podcasts. I write in my journal. I write down ten ideas. I write thank-you notes. Then I play with my kids and have breakfast.

After soaking up this boost of morning energy, I turn my attention to work. The first thing I do: all the low-energy tasks I don't want to do and couldn't delegate.

Already, I have two wins out of the way, a personal win because I got to spend the morning focused on gratitude and a professional win because I got the yuckies out of the way quickly. At this point, the day has still barely begun.

When you can rack up some wins early on, it makes everything else feel like a win too. It's like eating your vegetables first. I start my day by doing the stuff I don't want to do, and when it's done, I can be on fire for the rest of it. Those tasks don't weigh on my mind and hinder my creative mindset.

So how do you figure out what gives you energy? They're the things you do that don't make you tired. They don't exhaust you. You don't dread doing them. And when you do them, you actually want to do more.

Take Adam Gazda. Known simply as "Banana Beard" to fans (or as "Banana Bread" to one sweet old lady), Adam is a mighty manly maniac. And if you didn't guess by his nickname, his beard is shaped like a banana.

As big as his beard is, Adam's personality is even bigger. A competitive bearder (not to be confused with a competitive birder, which is a totally different thing), Adam is used to sculpting his formidable thatch into a variety of different shapes. So it was only natural that Adam would eventually become one of the Bananas' most visible fans.

The first time Adam donned his banana beard, it was on a dare. His friend called him up and said he had an extra ticket to the Bananas game. It was Adam's for the taking—but only on the condition that he do up his beard for the show. Challenge accepted.

The rest, as they say, is history.

Believe it or not, it only takes Adam about a half hour to whip his beard into shape: just part the beard down the middle, put a rubber band on the tip, and sculpt up the other side to get the full peel effect. Oh, and set it up as high as you can on your face. "I've learned that you always want to overstyle it because throughout the day it's going to fall a little bit," Adam says, noting the humid Savannah climate. "If you set it up high to start, it levels out by the end of the day."

Unsurprisingly, Bananas fans are deeply curious about all things Banana Beard. Does he wear it like that every day? (No. It's usually tucked into his shirt while he's at work.) Is it real? (Very much so.) Is it okay to touch it? (Only if you ask nicely.)

But there's one big question: why *does* he do it? What is it about being a Bananas fan that keeps him coming back? That gives him so much energy to sculpt—and wear—his artful beard time after time in the hot Southern summer?

It's the city, the people, the environment, Adam says. Bananas games are a safe place to be yourself without judgment. He may be the "beard guy," but everyone brings a part of themselves to the show. "If you're away from the circus, it's a bunch of crazy people doing crazy things. But once you're at the circus, you just blend in," Adam says. In other words, at Bananas games, you're free to let your freak flag fly.

Energy Audit

Think of a time when you had the best day or when you came home feeling great and energized. Why was that? What did you do that day that gave you energy? How can you change your schedule so you can do more of those things?

Now what about an exhausting day? What parts of your schedule feel like dreaded chores? What zaps your energy? Put the chores in the part of your day where they'll do the least damage to your energy. Or hire someone else who likes to do them!

Get Yourself Energized

"After all, I am a coach!"

—COACH RILEY

I have an "energy list" of all the things I love doing. I love being on podcasts. I love writing, creating, and doing new videos and promotions. I love reading and learning. I love giving keynotes. I love sharing the Bananas' story. Creating, sharing, and growing are my energizers. If I'm doing any of those three things in my day (such as writing this book), I have more energy at five o'clock than I do earlier in the day. They fire me up.

Not everyone is wired the same way. If they were to spend their day creating, sharing, and growing, they'd be exhausted because these activities aren't their passions. They don't give them energy. The point is still the same: fill your day with what gives you energy, and cut out the rest.

You might be thinking, *That's not fair, Jesse. I have to do the finances. I have to clean the house.* That's not true. You can hire an accountant, or you can hire a housekeeper. Hire or enlist people to do the things that don't give you energy so you can spend time doing the things that do. And when you're constantly energized, you'll be more successful and make more money.

If you have a scarcity mentality about money, this may be hard to accept, but think of the time and energy trade-off. Sure, it may cost extra to hire a lawn maintenance crew, but think of what you get for that expense—extra time to do something you love.

Again, the key is to find out what you are passionate about. As one of my favorite coaches likes to say, spend your time focusing on your "get-tos" rather than your "have-tos." You don't *have to* do anything.

Seven-year-olds are great at this.

Riley—or Coach Riley, as we call him—has loved the Bananas from day one of his first baseball camp. He loves cheering on the team. He loves participating in the promotions. He loves the players and the way they treat him like a brother. He especially loves Coach Gillum, who talks with him often during games about their three favorite things: baseball, players, and cowboy boots. "He's always been a Banana," Gillum says.

One day, Coach Gillum says Riley found his way past a normally locked fence into the dugout, acting "like he owned the place." There, he helped with warm-ups and then sat with Coach Gillum and the players and took in the game. Everyone was asking Coach Gillum who his mini-me was. Gillum said, "That's Riley, man. He just showed up—and now he runs the show." When his mom, Janna, went to retrieve him after the game, she found Riley on a chair next to Coach Gillum, who was doing a postgame interview. "I attribute this win to Coach Riley here," Coach Gillum said. "He made all the calls, and I just followed his lead!"

From that moment on, with all his heart and all his being, Riley was a coach for the Savannah Bananas, complete with a custom all-yellow jersey with "$\frac{1}{2}$" printed on the back.

As Coach Gillum's right-hand man, Riley handles all the important stuff. When the calls in the field don't go the Bananas' way, Riley calls for "umpire change-outs." He helps drag the field. He participates in intrateam dance rivalries. When he needs help with his homework or to brush up on his baseball signs, he consults Coach Gillum, morning and night, in person and online. Even during the height of the COVID-19 pandemic, Riley was at the practice field until ten at night helping out the players.

But then again, of course he was. "After all," Riley would say, "I *am* a coach!"

As part of his coaching duties, Riley and his family also regularly host Bananas players at their home, where Riley holds them to his very Fans First standard of "100 percent all-in on and off the field." The players are always happy to oblige, coaching neighborhood pick-up baseball games and even attending birthday parties.

Even a move across the state hasn't dampened Coach Riley's energy and commitment to the team—or their commitment to him. On the eve of Riley's departure, a player had a bat sent to Riley with the inscription, "There are no goodbyes, just see-you-laters. Joshua Keating #3 'Cowboy Keat.'"

Riley's energy and passion as a coach were infectious. Even as a seven-year-old, he inspired long-term friendships with everyone from professional coaches to college players he'd only met briefly.

All because he followed his get-tos.

Get Your Team Energized

"I don't know what that person went through that day. I don't know what they're going through in their lives. But if for just a few minutes I can make them forget about their problems, then it's worth it."

—MARTY JONES, THE MAIN MAN-NANA

Structure your business teams the same way as you structure your life. Make sure your people are spending time doing the things that give them energy. You can't do every task, and trying will only leave you behind, stressed, and depleted.

Some tasks will be have-tos, some will be get-tos. If you don't have the energy to do it and you don't have the right people for each role, the energy will run out. You have to place people where they will give and receive the most energy.

For Man-Nana Marty Jones, that place is front and center, leading the Bananas' all-male cheerleading squad.

From the moment Marty arrived at his first Bananas show in the summer of 2016, he was in shock. He thought he knew what a baseball game was all about: you sit through the first few innings. You laugh at a couple sponsored promotions. Then you get up, go to the bathroom, and walk around a little bit. Then you sneak out after the seventh-inning stretch and head home early so you can beat the traffic.

Marty had no reason to expect anything different from a summer college league team. In fact, he expected a lot less.

But this was different. From the second he arrived at Grayson, Marty says, the entertainment level was off the charts. And he wanted more. Soon, he was in the stands for the next Bananas game—and then the next, and then the next. Whenever he could get tickets (not always an easy thing to do), he was there.

Then came the costume—first the trademark oversized yellow glasses, then the hat, then the headband, and then the jerseys (he estimates he has over thirty). Finally, completing the ensemble are the ultra-rare yellow Chuck Taylor high-tops. "I had to go to a few different stores to get those," Marty says, with more than a hint of pride.

Marty had long-term experience in making people laugh. He had self-esteem issues when he was a kid related to his weight. He also moved to different schools. In order to adapt and nip any bullying in the bud, he turned to comedy as a way to entertain his peers and keep them on his side.

Even as he became more successful as an adult, the impulse to bring laughter to others stuck with him, "I would rather any day make someone laugh than make a dollar," Marty says. It's no surprise, then, that Marty was always the loudest and most active in his corner of Grayson—running up and down the aisles, hugging complete strangers, and leading chant after chant.

One day, just when Marty thought he had reached peak fan, his wife told him the Bananas were holding auditions for the

Man-Nanas, their all-male cheerleading squad. As fast as he could get his shoes on, Marty was at the audition—kicking, gyrating, and dropping it *low, low, low,* just like the song instructed him to.

From that day forward, Marty was a Man-Nana.

Easiest decision we ever had to make.

Marty is dedicated to the Bananas. When we went on our One City World Tour to Mobile in 2021, Marty cut his family vacation short (with gracious permission from his wife) to hop on a bus with us the moment he got back to Savannah. We totally would have understood if he couldn't make it, but as he said, he wanted to be part of "Bananas history."

But Marty isn't just part of Bananas history. He's a star. Just ask the people of Mobile. The day after the game, he was already a legend, with people stopping him in the streets and thanking him for the show. "I was proud of that," Marty says. "Not proud because I was there and I did something. I was proud because I knew we created some joy in that community."

But why do it? Why put all this energy into being a Bananas fan? To Marty, it's all about the people, their reactions, and making their days a little bit better. "I don't know what that person went through that day. I don't know what they're going through in their lives," he says. "But if for just a few minutes, I can make them forget about their problems, then it's worth it."

Fans First to Marty means, "Nobody leaves disappointed."

Ultimately, that's the point of being a Man-Nana to Marty. And for that reason alone, he's happy to do it. But the recognition is nice too. Whether it's going viral on the Bananas' TikTok channel ("My man is a *star*," his wife said of the clip) or getting profiled in *Entrepreneur*, Marty is all for it. "I'd always wanted to be in *Entrepreneur* magazine," Marty says with a laugh, "but I never thought it would be as a male cheerleader."

GET UP AND LEAD

"I got up that first game because I believed in myself. You've got to cheer yourself on first. If you do, the crowd will cheer you on. The cheer you give is the cheer you get."

—CAMERON HUGHES

Cameron Hughes is the King of Cheer, the Sultan of Celebration, the World's *Only* Professional Fan. He's crazy, over the top, an idea machine, a ball of energy who's all about bringing the fun.

Here's an idea of what Cameron's like, even when he's not leading the cheer. After my first-ever call with Cameron, I sent him a pair of Dolce and Banana underwear as a thank you for his time.

A few days later, I was eating dinner with my family when I got a FaceTime call. It was Cameron—and he was wearing the underwear on his face. Noticing we were all eating, he proceeded to put on a show, making faces at my son, Maverick, who was beside himself with laughter.

Then, when I got to Grayson Stadium the next day, I saw Cameron had another surprise for me: a bunch of bananas. Well, more like several bunches of bananas. I shipped his underwear. He shipped my bananas.

Again, this is just Cameron's baseline. When he's onstage, he's everything I just described dialed up to a hundred and eleven.

It started for Cameron at an Ottawa hockey game in 1994. No one was cheering. Cameron was upset. People paid money for this game. He eventually couldn't stand it anymore and—despite a vigorous "Don't do it" from his friend—got up on his seat to dance during a rousing rendition of "We Are Family." The crowd got into his performance. Those closest to him started to cheer. Then play resumed, and Cameron sat back down.

That could have been the end of it.

But at the next break in play, ten thousand people turned to look at him. The DJ even put on a big dance song. At this point, Cameron was thinking, *What do I do? They want me to do something. I've got to do something.*

So he got up and started dancing up and down the aisle, flailing his arms like one of those skinny balloon people at a used car lot. The crowd lost their mind, rising as one in a standing ovation.

The next day, after he got home from his uneventful hockey rink job, his dad showed him the front page of the Ottawa newspaper:

"Dancing Redhead Bandit Steals the Show at Senators Game." Soon, the team reached out to him to come back for the next game—and the game after that and the game after that (and so on), and Cameron's career as a professional fan was launched.

In the decades since, Cameron has traveled all over the world, igniting crowds from the NBA Finals to the US Open. He's been hired by over twenty-five professional sports leagues in eleven countries and performed at two Olympic Games. All in all, he's performed for over twenty-five million people.

But why? What is it about being a fan that Cameron likes so much? "I got up that first game because I believed in myself," Cameron says. "You've got to cheer on yourself first. If you do, the crowd will cheer you on. That's the most valuable message that I lived and want to share with people. It has to start from the heart. You can't look to your left and your right anymore for permission because at a certain point, you're going to grow up and you're going to have to make these decisions."

For Cameron, being your own biggest fan is about getting up on the seat of your own life in ways that celebrate your talent and spirit. It's letting loose the best of you where others can see it. That's what makes you thrive.

Be remembered for who you are, not for what you've accomplished.

Being your own biggest fan, then, means taking care of yourself first before taking care of others. For Banana Beard, that means getting only mustard on his ballpark hotdog so no uncomplementary colors get smeared into his beard. For Coach Riley, that may mean doing his homework before practice so the rest of the day is free to party. For Marty the Man-Nana, that means setting his cheerleading costume out four hours early—just because he's excited about putting it back on again.

For all of them, it's being true to yourself and giving your spirit what it needs to flourish.

Self-Care

If you want to be your own biggest fan, what will you do for yourself? How will you eliminate friction in your life? How will you entertain yourself? How will you experiment with new things that bring you joy? How will you engage deeply with what matters to you? How will you engage deeply with someone else? You can't live in isolation; you have to engage people in new and different ways. Finally, how will you empower your own action on these things? How will you get up out of your seat?

GET UP AND BECOME

"I hope my story will inspire you to cheer a little louder, smile a little wider, dance a little crazier, contribute to your team, be fearless and most importantly, to GET UP and become your biggest fan!"

—CAMERON HUGHES

The biggest competition for customer experience should be yourself. How can your own experience be better tomorrow than it was today? If you continually seek to become, then you will be playing the game that you should be playing and not competing against others.

The message of this chapter is simple: love what you do, and do what you love. Be kind to yourself. Be passionate. Be proud. Organize your day so you get to be the best version of yourself, and do those things that bring you joy and energy.

To be your own biggest fan, don't be afraid to ask for what you need and want—and to put your passions out into the world for everyone to see. Judgment only works if you feel ashamed.

If a twenty-something red-haired Canadian can dance on his seat.

If a staff member dressed like a leprechaun can give the speech of his life.

If a guy can sculpt his beard into a banana.

If a seven-year-old can coach a baseball team.

If a middle-aged, full-figured businessman can be a male cheer-leader.

You can definitely be the leader you want to be.

And the best way to free up your time and energy to grow into that person and that life is to build a team around you that can do and *likes* to do the stuff you hate. That can infuse your business with loads of their own positive energy. That can run the ship when you're not there.

So how do you build that team of superfans? Well, I'm glad you asked.

The Bananas Bookshelf

The Miracle Morning: The Not-So-Obvious Secret Guaranteed to Transform Your Life (Before 8AM) by Hal Elrod

Innovation Secrets of Steve Jobs by Carmine Gallo

King of Cheer by Cameron Hughes

BUILD A TEAM OF SUPERFANS

"Make your people proud. We want Disney to be the most admired company."

—BOB IGER

One summer night at Grayson Stadium, it was President Jared's turn to play undercover fan. To add a little extra fun to the proceedings, he decided to bring his family with him.

Not too long into the show, his sister asked, "Who's that guy pushing the cart down the first base side?"

Jared looked over. It was Reginald, the star of our maintenance crew.

Everyone on our team knows Reginald (and many of our fans do too). Reginald is an all-around amazing person—one of our favorite people—who has one of the hardest jobs in the ballpark: keeping the place clean. Still, he shows up for work every day with a smile on his face, radiating pure energy and giving every-one elbows. Even when it's about to rain, he says, "It's a great day for baseball!" He's just the happiest guy in the world.

It was that energy that first caught the attention of Jared's sister. Forget the promotions, the players, and the rest of the spectacle that was going on around her. She noticed the guy taking out the trash—not because he was doing anything wrong but because his love for the job made him stand out.

From the moment the city announced we were taking over Grayson Stadium in 2015, Reginald was determined to join our crew, calling us every week to see if we had any positions open. He just really wanted to work for us. Finally, we had a few conversations with him, quickly realized he was one of us, and happily told him he was on the team as our first part-time employee. He's still with us to this day.

What a great decision that was.

Reginald embodies a core tenet of the Fans First Way. It doesn't matter who you are on the team—the Stadium Operations Coordinator, an intern, or a maintenance worker. We all impact our fans. We all work together to create an unforgettable expe-rience. Therefore, we are all important, integral members of a team that keeps this company successful.

Your team can't create fans if they are not fans themselves. You can't do what you don't know. The most important step in getting your company shipshape (or banana-shape) is to grow a culture that legitimately cares about the outcome of your busi-ness. They have to want to own the ship.

The best way to do that? Build a team of superfans. To go Fans First, you must take care of your First Fans. If you can do that, then you won't have to worry about running the ship—the ship will run itself.

That's exactly what we did for Reginald. During our second season, Reginald told me his birthday was on a game day. Actually, he told everyone—the front office staff, the coaches, even the players. It was clear he wanted us to know how special this day was to him. We couldn't just ignore that.

So during our team pep rally, we sang "Happy Birthday." We had balloons and a cake. "For me?" Reginald yelled. *Of course* it was for him, after he told everyone!

He was ecstatic, but we weren't done.

"Hey, Reginald, one more thing," I said. "Can you make sure to be in the dugout right before the game starts?"

"Sure thing. Whatever you need. I'll be there," he said.

Soon it was game time. As the announcer went through the lineup, the players ran down the line, the pep band swirled, and everyone got fired up and ready for the game.

Then, over the loudspeaker, the announcer said, "You know him. You love him. Let's hear it for...Reginald!"

Without a moment's hesitation, Reginald threw his arms up in the air and ran down the line, high-fiving every single player as he went. At the end of the line, the team was waiting for him with a jersey with his name on it. As he put on his jersey and lined up with the team, a single tear ran down his face. He said it was amazing, that it was the best day of his life.

Was it really worth it to go the extra mile for Reginald? Absolutely, one hundred percent, without a doubt, yes. What we did truly mattered to him, which meant it mattered to us.

But still, we weren't done.

Flash forward to the 2021 season. The players wanted Reginald in the dugout as a coach. He went all in, even taking it upon himself to provide that bit of extra oomph with targeted pep talks.

"All right, guys. Very important. Don't swing at anything unnecessary." Solemnly, the hitters all nodded their heads. Good advice, Reginald. Good advice.

In his first year as a coach, the team went all the way to the CPL championship. In front of a sold-out crowd, the Bananas recorded the last out to win it all, and the players handed the trophy to Reginald. The whole stadium chanted his name.

Talk about an unforgettable experience—and not just for Reginald. For everyone in that stadium. For the players. For the team. For me.

All of us superfans. Fanatics. Not just about the game but about each other. In order to understand the fans, you have to know what it feels like to be one. We help our people feel like the fans. We recognize their hard work. All the wacky stories you've heard in this book? It takes a lot of effort to create those. We also know how good it feels to experience them, which is why we make sure our team knows just how much we value them.

So how do you create superfans out of your First Fans?

Well, it's not by getting them bit by a radioactive banana.

It's by caring about them as you would any fan. Eliminate friction from their jobs. Entertain them. Empower their ideas. Engage with what they love, and experiment with ways to recognize and appreciate their hard work.

It's by keeping your First Fans First.

ELIMINATE FRICTION: MAKE YOUR TEAM'S JOB EASIER

"It doesn't matter who you are, what your race is, what your religion is. It doesn't matter where you come from. It doesn't matter where you're going. Every single person, when they walk onto this team, becomes a unit. Everyone's here for one reason, and they leave for the same reason. They're happy they came and happy to come back. It's amazing knowing that everything in the world that's going on is completely forgotten when people are here. No one worries about anything else while they're in the stadium."

—JOHNATHAN WALTERS,
BANANAS STADIUM OPERATIONS COORDINATOR

One of the first things to do to build a team of superfans is to get rid of the things that make your team members' jobs harder and more tedious.

From the get-go, get rid of policies. As I've said before, policies police, and that instills a culture of fear, not love. We don't have any policies. We don't have a rulebook or a handbook. We don't have any rules about dress code or taking vacation time. We trust everyone to be an adult. Some people may view this as being irresponsible or weak, but to us, it's freedom. And everyone wants freedom in their jobs. Again, people don't want to be managed; they want to be led.

We don't need policies because there is a better, more trusting, loving, engaging way to guide your team.

Instead of policies, we focus on mindset and outcomes. The mindset is Fans First, and the outcome we want to see is making people feel good. This may sound like a cat poster, but it works.

Another common employee hurdle is the annual review.

We don't do annual reviews. We do quarterly check-ins. And these meetings don't center around performance; they're all about checking in on our people. While we might discuss their job, we're more interested in finding out how they're doing. We want them to know we care more about them as a person than an employee.

Again, this practice is supportive rather than punitive. It rewards not punishes. It brings people closer together instead of splitting them apart. And it's just one more thing that makes our people incredibly dedicated and loyal.

ENTERTAIN ALWAYS: THE *FIRST* FIRST FAN EXPERIENCE

"People who spend money with us aren't buying tickets to a baseball game—they're spending their money to be a part of something fun and bizarre and wholesome, to suspend life for a moment, to be at the ballpark and laugh and sing and dance. Whether it's for thirty games over the course of a summer or for a few hours on a family vacation, people want to feel like they belong, and we have the opportunity to provide that for lots of people."

—CARSON BOWEN,
BANANAS TICKET EXPERIENCE COORDINATOR

Think back to a time when you started a new job. You showed up and got onboarded, and then you headed home. Inevitably, someone asked you, "Well, how was your first day?" What did you say in return? I'll take a guess: "It was fine."

That's not a very good answer.

But even then, it's better than the answer I gave my first day interning for a baseball team. That experience was anything but fine—it was terrifying. I walked in, and they threw a phone book and a price sheet at me and said, "Start calling."

I had no idea what they meant. There was no coaching, teaching, training, or any of that. I had to figure it out all on my own. Eventually I did, but that didn't make that first day any less bewildering.

Throughout this book, we've talked about the importance of first impressions. To make sure we give everyone our best energy and attention, we treat everyone as if it's their first game. For our First Fans—our team members—we also believe in the importance of the first day. So we make it our mission to make that first day be a complete celebration of the new team member.

Whether it's a new intern or a part-time or full-time team member, we throw them a party—fully scripted, of course. As soon as they show up, we're all there to greet them, decked out in full costumes. We play music, throw confetti, shoot silly string, the works. They get Bananas shirts. They get their favorite drinks and snacks. They get to feel loved and appreciated from day one.

From there, we spend the morning setting expectations on what's going to happen over the next few days. Then, we take them out to lunch. We ask them how they like to be appreciated, and we do questionnaires and quizzes to find out more about them. Finally, after going through some more onboarding, we celebrate our new team member again as they're getting ready to head out the door. We do cheers, and they get their picture on the wall.

The goal is to make this first day as memorable as possible, just as we'd want for any of our fans. We don't ever want our team members to forget their first Fans First Moment and what it is like to be part of our team. Not only does this help them feel good and start building relationships (which is the most important thing), but it also gets them talking. That way, when someone asks them what their first day was like, they don't just say, "It was fine." They rave about the experience. They have so much to say they don't even know where to begin.

They have a good story. And that sets the tone for the rest of their time with us. It puts them on the path to becoming a superfan.

By going Fans First for our First Fans, even new hires seem to instinctively get what we're all about even on the first day. Take Bananas Director of Entertainment Zack Frongillo. We first reached out to Zack ahead of the 2021 season because we were looking for a new entertainment lead to run the show. It was just a seasonal position, I explained, but Zack was interested anyway, and he agreed to fly out to Savannah and audition with us for our Banana Ball spring games.

On Zack's very first day, he asked to speak to all the players and team to plan and rehearse the script. He addressed everyone confidently and then said, "Let's bring it in." Everyone huddled together and Zack said, "Fans First on three! One, two, three!"

All the players and entertainment team yelled, "Fans First!"

In all my years, we've never broken it down to Fans First. Yet this person auditioning on their first day brought the team together and led a Fans First cheer as if he'd been part of the Bananas for years. He knew that Fans First was everything, and he was already ready to give everything to the Fans First Way.

Needless to say, Zack got the job—a job that quickly went from seasonal to permanent.

Nervous? Who's Nervous?

"I was nervous on my first day. I didn't know what I was stepping into on the other side of our yellow door or if the Bananas were really what they appeared to be. Then I stepped into the office lobby to every Bananas employee in costume—Matt as Mr. Incredible, Jared as Dorothy, a chicken that might have been Lizzy, a Kara Heater avocado, and someone who had a cannon as Barney the Friendly Dinosaur, pelting me with foam baseballs, confetti poppers, and expired silly string. I knew it was expired because it stuck and ruined my shirt, but I didn't care at all—I was a freakin' Banana, baby."

—CARSON BOWEN, TICKET EXPERIENCE DIRECTOR

EMPOWER ACTION: SUPPORT YOUR TEAM'S GROWTH

"I'm a fan because I can bust out in song, do weird accents, and dance in the office and people don't laugh at me; they simply join in."

—KARA HEATER,
BANANAS DIRECTOR OF MARKETING AND ATTENTION

Emily Cole believes being Fans First starts with just "being a good human." She highlights how coaching good behavior starts during the hiring process. "This gives us a chance to really work alongside someone and show them how things operate in Bananaland. If they can naturally mirror the way we treat people, that's the first requirement. We can coach the skills part."

For example, we send handwritten thank-you cards to people who interview for full-time positions. If we get a handwritten thank-you card back, it's a great indicator that they listen carefully and respond. It also means they can pick up our culture's language. "When great individuals join our team, they automatically become even more caring, different, enthusiastic, fun, growing, and hungry because that's the Fans First Way, and that's what we focus on daily," Emily emphasizes.

These little tests may sound like a lot to do just to be hired, but people love our interview process. It has three parts. First, applicants do a video cover letter so we can see their personality. (Coach Gillum's was legendary, helping him to beat out a coach from MLB's Pittsburgh Pirates.) Second, they write a Fans First essay and explain how they fit our core beliefs. Third, they write a future resume because we're more interested in what they'd like to do in the future than what they've already done.

This last part leads to deeper engagement with our new team member. We ask our staff members what they want to do in the future so we can work toward those goals and better support them. We can have open conversations about their goals. We may hire them to work for the Bananas, but we also want what's best for them as opposed to what's best for us. We acknowledge that it's not all about us, that they are not living just for this company, and that they are still their own separate people, with their own hopes and dreams and creativity.

If this means your team member eventually leaves to join another team, then so be it. In fact, we even help team members find jobs elsewhere—just like we did for Austin the Awkward Rapper. If that was the best way to support his dreams, we were happy to do it. Emily even wrote him a send-off poem on his last day. Here are the last two stanzas:

> He holds down the plaza like no other and we'll always consider him our cigar-smoking brother.

> Austin, we are ecstatic about this opportunity and are so proud of you Call us when you're back in Savannah so we can catch up over a cold brew.

Sometimes doing the best for your team means watching them go somewhere else. But a lot of our interns or seasonal workers tend to stick around. Other "former" team members stay involved with the Bananas or stay on with us part time. Berry Aldridge, for instance, gave us plenty of notice that he was leaving...but then he chose to stay with us in a new role as our Baseball Operations Coordinator. Ben Sheffield started as an intern and after a few years became the mastermind behind all our videos. He left for a position in a new city but stayed on part time so he could still be part of Bananaland. Others continue to grow with the team in new directions. Take Johnathan Walters, for example. Johnathan joined on as a parking penguin because he needed extra money to help take care of his mom. At six-four, Johnathan was taller than our average parking penguin, but the suit fit, and he was determined to make the best out of it.

Soon, he was making quite an impression on fans as he happy-footed around the parking lot, directing people where to park. And even early on, Johnathan was committed to living up to the Fans First promise. When he noticed that we didn't have enough handicap parking spaces, he immediately took his concerns to the front office team. A week later, there was a whole new row of spots right next to the Stadium Club lot.

His role with the Bananas only grew from there. During his second and third seasons, Johnathan bartended for our Top Bar and Stadium Club. He enjoyed the work, but what he really wanted to get more involved. So in 2020, Johnathan began an internship with us in the front office.

What a year to be an intern. Almost immediately after starting, the world locked down as a result of the COVID-19 pandemic, and Johnathan was left to perform most of his tasks at home.

As you already know, the Bananas found plenty of ways to connect with fans during the lockdowns. But Johnathan wanted more. So he found a bunch of the specialty liquor we used to make our signature drink, the Slippery Banana—which, according to Johnathan, tastes "like Laffy Taffy that's been soaked in liquor for three months." Then, we got permission from the proper authorities (to-go drinks had been legalized during quarantine), broke out the Mason jars, and opened a Slippery Banana drive-through for fans.

On the first day, about fifty came though, and we sold out our supply in twenty-five minutes.

On the second day, Johnathan and his team kicked it up a notch. Split was out there. There were tents selling merch items like bandanas, hats, T-shirts, and balls. Our shiny new bike racks with the Bananas logo glistened in the sun. This time, cars were lined up over an hour before we even opened. About forty-five minutes and three hundred cars later, we were sold out again.

On the third day, it was pouring rain. But by this point, you know that a little rain can't keep a good Banana down. Drenched as they were, Johnathan and his team kept dancing around without a care in the world, serving Slippery Bananas to car after car.

To Johnathan, that drive-through was the best. "It's really heartwarming to know that even through a pandemic, people still wanted to come see us. People still wanted to come and have our product and feel like they were part of the Bananas."

After crushing it as a parking penguin, a bartender, and a (bartending) intern, Johnathan stepped in full time as our Stadium Operations Coordinator, filling the departing Jonathan Wood's shoes. (Jonathan Wood, by the way, gave us six months' notice when he and his wife decided to move closer to their families and then personally hired and trained his replacement).

Through all this growth and change, Johnathan has remained a Bananas superfan. But more importantly, he's always ready to step in and do whatever needs to be done to create the most Fans First experience possible.

These days, Johnathan is responsible for running all the stadium bars, concessions, equipment, and setup for the ballpark. As a parking penguin, he directed tens of people. Now he directs thousands. He's even managed to finesse operations to improve our all-you-can-eat service. "I've learned that I'm stronger, I smarter, and more important than I ever thought I was going to be," Johnathan says. "For the first time, when I started working here, it made me feel whole, made me feel special, made me feel like I was really going to be a part of something special one day."

And that, my friends, is empowerment.

ENGAGE DEEPLY: LEARN, LOVE, AND RECOGNIZE

"I never thought I would consider anywhere other than my small town in Texas home. But now when I say home, I'm talking about Savannah, and it's all because of the friends I've made at the Bananas that have become my family."

—SAVANAH ALANIZ,
BANANAS MARKETING COORDINATOR

Fans First Director Marie Matzinger is a big fan of Gary Chapman's book *The Five Love Languages*. In it, Chapman explains that we have different emotional and relational needs. And if we can understand both our needs and the needs of others, we can interact with them more effectively and grow stronger relationships. According to Chapman, the five love languages are words of affirmation, physical touch, receiving gifts, acts of service, and quality time.

After learning about the five love languages, Marie was determined to bring this conversation to the team with the goal of creating a sense of self-awareness and team awareness. Over the following weeks, we learned a lot about each other and our love languages. For example, Emily's love language is acts of service. Jared's love language is words of affirmation. He likes being appreciated by being told what he did well. But don't you dare touch him.

Jonathan Wood's love language is also words of affirmation. When Jonathan left the team, Marie put together a book of thank–you notes from everyone, saying what Jonathan meant to them. Then, he gave a speech about how much the Bananas and everyone meant to him. He was crying, and everyone in the place was crying. Even interns who'd been with us for one month were crying.

Everyone was all-in in that moment, even during a goodbye, which doesn't always happen in business circles. Just from us showing that we'd listened, cared, and responded creatively.

To create a team of superfans, listening, caring, and responding creatively are what it's all about. The five love languages is one way we learn to recognize our team, but another way is through the daily dose of recognition. This practice shows every team member that what they do is noticed and important. It also highlights how we serve each other, building that team relationship.

> Stop looking to be recognized, and start looking
> to recognize.

Every staff meeting begins with this daily dose. We open the discussion up for leads and staff to give shoutouts that notice the good things team members have done. We also have a "Shout Out Central" channel on Microsoft Teams where we post shoutouts from staff and fans alike. In either case, the key here is to be specific, and it's best when the person who witnessed the good deed does the recognizing.

Personally, one of my favorite ways to engage deeply with our superfans is to send handwritten letters to the parents of new team members. These letters only take a few moments to write, and they give me a chance to recognize those parents, thank them for raising such an amazing human being, let them know what a great culture fit their child is, and reassure them we are going to care for them like family.

This started when our then-twenty-four-year-old president, Jared Orton, wrote cards to the parents of the three twenty-two-year-olds we hired to launch the team with us in 2015. These kids were taking a big risk. They all moved to Georgia right out of school to work for a startup. It was gutsy, and Jared wanted the parents to know that we were going to protect them and care for them. As we've grown, our leadership team now takes turns writing to the parents of staff and interns. We do it because it's the right thing to do, but also because it creates some really important fans along the way: mom and dad.

Finally, we also tell our team when fans recognize them. Marie, who manages all fan love and communication, collects fan-written recognitions from our online contact forms and shared with me the following example. A fan shared how their father, who had been experiencing the onset of dementia, had trouble finding his way back to his seat after using the bathroom. The usher recognized what was going on and helped him back to his seat. Not only did the usher help throughout that game, but he also continued to help at future games. The family greatly appreciated this. We recognized the usher in front of our team with a thank-you note and gift card.

Marie is proud of the way we appreciate our team: "The recognition in front of your peers is something that we do pretty well. It encourages people to live out those Fans First stories. It's not just lip service—it's stuff that is really happening, and it doesn't go unnoticed."

Support No Matter What

"What stands out are the moments when things are hard. I lost my father during the 2017 season. I did not show up to work for a single day from July until September. I had to help keep my family's business afloat while dealing with the loss of a parent. Never once did I receive a text asking when I was coming back. It was not 'Where are you?' It was 'What can we do for you?' These were more than coworkers and bosses. Everyone was there for me when I needed it most, and I will never forget it.

Gifts and things are easy, but when you truly need someone is when you find out who people are. I am beyond
proud to be a part of this team because I know when
anyone here needs us, every person here will be willing
to step up."

–PATRICK BRIODY, BANANAS WORLD TOUR DIRECTOR

EXPERIMENT CONSTANTLY: GIVE BACK TO YOUR TEAM

*"When you believe in a thing, believe in it implicitly
and unquestionably."*

—WALT DISNEY

A big part of showing your team how much you recognize and
appreciate them is to spend some company money on them.
They helped earn it, after all, so they should also get to celebrate
with it. Experiment to find out what are actually meaningful as
gifts, and keep those offerings fresh and surprising. Boring old
pizza parties need not apply.

To afford this experimentation, we've established a One Percent
Rule (yes, rules are bad, except this one). We allocate 1 percent
of our top line for Surprise and Delight moments for our team.
I strongly believe every company should do this. If you're a $5
million company, that means you have $50,000 right there

to spend on your team. If you make $2 million a year, that's $20,000 for team surprises. Besides, that $20,000 isn't considered profit since it's taken from the top line.

In other words, this isn't about finding money in the budget. It's about having it and giving it, no matter what. By including team care money in the budget, we don't have to ask permission to do these things. We don't have to worry about taking money from other areas. We don't have to fret about whether or not we can do it. It's in the budget, so it's easy. It's formal and official. It eliminates friction around how we spend our money.

And with this allocated money, we can give amazing gifts of appreciation to our team. Gifts that actually mean something to the person being recognized.

Here are a few of Emily and my favorites. She wrote parts of these stories, so just imagine the "we" here is both our voices together. Call us Jessily.

The Cruise

At the beginning of 2016, we were $1.8 million in debt and sleeping on an air bed, but we worked hard, sold out every single game, won the CPL championship, and finished with a profitable season. It was a lot to go through, but we made it.

To celebrate our accomplishment, Emily wanted to do something special for our team, so we decided to take all of them and a plus-one for each on a cruise. We told Jared, and he was all-in too. Most of the staff had never been on a cruise—or even out of the country, for that matter. Not only would this cruise be an amazing gesture, but it would also be an amazing opportunity to get to know some of the special people in their lives.

Now, all we had to do was think of a fun way to share the news.

Before the last playoff game, we brought everyone into the visiting locker room. We had a bunch of beach balls, and Jared and Emily wore Hawaiian shirts. Emily had originally planned to be the one to tell everyone about the cruise, but she couldn't. She was too overcome with emotion to make the announcement, so Jared stepped up. Emily ended up just throwing beach balls in the air and bringing the energy.

Sure, a cruise might not seem like the biggest deal, but it was a reflection of how far we'd come in such a short amount of time. College summer league teams don't usually do well enough to take their teams on cruises—especially not after their first season. But we got there because of all the teamwork, effort, and energy that everyone put in.

Our team stuck with us through a lot of trial, error, and uncertainty. Giving back was a chance to replenish not only our own spirit but theirs.

The Party Bus

Dave Ramsey's Entreleadership team shut down a mall in Nashville, Tennessee, so their employees could go on a shopping spree around Christmas. It was all a total surprise. One moment, the employees were working. The next moment, they had the run of the mall. After hearing that story, we did something in the same spirit.

Jared called a staff meeting. For the first several minutes, he talked about our vision and how we had to stick to it even in challenging times. Then, he began talking about how we always put our team first and continued to do unexpected things to surprise them.

At that, he said, "Okay, team. Clear your schedules. Clear your desks. We're leaving in thirty minutes."

The team had no idea what he was talking about. But he had their full attention. As they started packing up, the catered Chick-fil-A breakfast arrived. Then the party bus pulled up. No one knew where we were going, but everyone got on anyway.

After enjoying our mimosas and Chick-fil-A in the limo, we parked in front of Tanger Outlets. We gave every person on the team a five-hundred-dollar gift card, and they went shopping.

For some team members, this little gift was a much-needed shopping spree. Johnathan Walters, for instance, bought three new pairs of shoes to replace the shabby old ones that were literally falling apart on his feet. He dumped the old ones on the spot and put a new pair on.

Dream Trip

When Marie first came onboard, her family was skeptical of her joining the Bananas on the heels of her successful academic career. All they saw was a failing team in its startup phase that no one knew anything about. Why take such a big risk right out of college, especially for only $25,000 a year?

We lived past that first year, thanks in large part to Marie's leadership. Soon, she became our Finance Director and then the Fans First Director.

Fans First Director is the role Marie was born for. Why? Because she's both practical *and* caring. She'll read a book like *The Five Love Languages* and immediately ask how she can bring that to the business.

And she's always asking questions. What's your favorite food? What's on your bucket list? What trips do you want to take? She engages. She listens, and she acts. She brings us closer together as a team.

In 2018, after an especially challenging year in which she had to balance multiple roles, we decided we had to show her our gratitude in a big way. We knew Marie's dream trip was to go to Ireland, so we decided it was finally time to make that happen.

And of course, we had to make a big reveal of it. So we invited her to a team celebration dinner. As the night progressed, Emily got everyone's attention and began reading a poem she'd written about Marie's time with us and all her accomplishments. At the end came the big reveal: Marie was going to Ireland for a full week! As we handed her catalogs about Ireland and a six-pack of Guinness, she broke out into happy tears.

And you know who she took to Ireland? The person who was most skeptical about her job with the Bananas years prior: her father. Marie says their memories from that trip will last a lifetime.

Team Care

We've all heard about self-care. The Bananas also practice team care.

Whenever we can, we try to do little Surprise and Delight moments with our team. A breakfast buffet with mimosas, fluffy slippers, massage therapists, car detailing, food trucks...whatever it takes to make our team feel pampered and appreciated.

In 2020, though, COVID-19 put the usual luxuries out of reach. For a little while there, a grocery run was about the biggest luxury anyone could expect—although our team would have never expected us to go on grocery runs for them.

So that's exactly what we did. We took a day and went grocery shopping—filling bags with food ranging from practical to pranky to pranktical (yep, that's a word now). Then, we took the ding-dong-deliver-and-dash approach. In other words, we went to all fourteen full-time team members' homes, dropped the groceries in front of their doors, rang the doorbells, and hightailed it out of there.

To add a final special touch, Emily wrote a poem for each team member and placed it in their bag. Each one ended with the same last two lines:

In times of uncertainty, we have to stay positive and thrive
So we hope this ridiculous delivery makes you feel alive!

Sometimes it's just the little things. Even a few Kit-Kats, some mac 'n' cheese, and some fresh veggies can go a long way in saying how much your superfans mean to you.

YOU CAN BE A LEADER HERE: THE SUPERFAN

"Leadership sets the example. There are times when they work harder than the staff, but they're always out there with smiles on their faces, looking like they're having a great time. You can tell everyone on the team has the same sense of purpose, and they love what they do. Leadership wants us to grow to greater heights, and I believe all staff feels the same way."

—JOHNATHAN WALTERS,
BANANAS STADIUM OPERATIONS COORDINATOR

Marie likes to say that culture is reflected from the top down. Leadership sets the tone. They are the role models. They are the ones who will put their own dreams on hold to make sure the team has everything it needs to be successful. By showing loyalty to your team, your team takes that loyalty and amplifies it tenfold. You don't have to be best friends with every single person on the team, but you have to have their backs.

To show our people we put them first, we invest heavily in them, not just with money but with our time, expertise, and resources. You can't pay your staff a low wage, have a work environment that sucks, and then tell them to take care of the fans. It won't work. Just like in the movie *Office Space,* if you're telling your employees they need fifteen pieces of flair in a flairless work environment, you're headed for a reckoning. If you don't treat your team like superfans, they won't be.

Jared always has the same message for all new interns and team members on their first day: you can be a leader here. You have an opportunity to impact people's lives in ways that you haven't yet imagined. Look for opportunities to lead, and you will find them.

This was a lesson Jared had to learn for himself. When he was younger, Jared used to think that being part of a ballclub was all about selling tickets or sponsorships and making money for the team. Now, he says, "That responsibility is so much more important and rewarding because I realize the impact I've been able to make on people inside and outside of our organization."

These aren't just empty words. They're the key to understanding why the Bananas didn't just survive over their first few seasons but flourished. It's not just about doing business but about making an impact.

To that, the first thing you can do as a leader is to change your mindset.

It's easy to think of all the reasons you shouldn't succeed. You don't have the skills. You don't have the team. You don't have the infrastructure. You don't have the resources. You don't have the money. You just sold your house and are sleeping on an air mattress. (Okay, maybe that last one was specific to Emily and me).

But are those obstacles insurmountable? Is what you're trying to do actually impossible or just difficult? Do you really mind being called an outsider?

For the Bananas, the answer wasn't looking at our problems and feeling bad for ourselves. It was remembering the promise we made to each other, to our fans, and to our *First Fans*. With that as our focus, we committed to getting just one person to love us—and then another and another. Eventually, we had built enough love to fill Grayson Stadium every night.

When you care for your people, they'll care for your fans, and your fans will take care of your bottom line.

If this sounds like something you want for your business, then Marie has just one word of advice: "Don't wait. Go ahead and do something. Start with one little thing for one person, and see how it feels. And then regardless of reaction or response, do it again for somebody else. And again and again and again. As soon as you start doing it, it's going to start a snowball effect for your business and in your relationships and then your relationship with your fans."

The Bananas Bookshelf

Fully Staffed: The Definitive Guide to Finding and Keeping Great Employees by Eric Chester

Raving Fans: A Revolutionary Approach to Customer Service by Ken Blanchard and Sheldon Bowles

Super Fans: The Easy Way to Stand Out, Grow Your Tribe, and Build a Successful Business by Pat Flynn

9:30 p.m.

SPREAD THE LOVE

"People can't love you if they don't know you."

—PAT FLYNN

When we went to Mobile, Alabama for our first-ever One City World Tour, everything was brand-new again. Here we were, in a city that didn't know who we were, that had never seen us play, that had never experienced one of our shows.

It felt just like the early days in Savannah. A new team with a new show in a new town—and totally unsure how to get the word out.

We sold out both shows—seven thousand tickets—before we came to town. The first night sold out in twenty-four hours. It was a bit...fanatical.

But how? How could we sell out both games in an entirely new city so quickly? How did the fans know to show up early for the show, to wear their custom Bananas gear, to be ready for the show of their lives?

Simple. Our reputation preceded us.

The Bananas have fans all around the United States—all around the world. And if there's one thing you can say about Bananas fans, it's that they aren't shy about flying their fan flag. So when we announced that we were coming to Mobile, those fans made sure everyone they knew in Mobile (and surrounding states) knew we were coming.

Once the early birds started buying tickets, that was all the momentum we needed. Then, when the first show sold out, we made a big deal of that, knowing that the best way to attract attention is to tell people something is completely sold out.

Then, with so much hype surrounding the games, it felt only natural to show up early. This new crop of fans knew they were in for something special, and they didn't want to miss a second of it.

The love this new city showed us was mind-blowing.

I got misty-eyed all weekend. I couldn't believe we had this many fans in a totally different city. In a totally different state! It was energizing. On closing night in Mobile, I was like a skinny, yellow tux-wearing version of Ric Flair. But I felt like I'd won the World Series. Like I'd won over the world.

I've hit three home runs in a game. I've pitched no-hitters. I even got to pitch at Fenway. I've done things that are really cool on a baseball field. Nothing was as cool as that night when all our hard work and wild ideas became reality. It was one of the best moments I've ever had in a stadium.

You've heard our story. You've learned all about the Five Es that we live by to create an unforgettable experience. You've seen the importance of not only being your biggest fan but also taking care of your First Fans—your team.

Here is the payoff. When you have everything working for you—the vision, the Five Es, the Fans First focus—then you never need to sell a day in your life. Instead, you get to do something much more important (and much more fun): you get to spread the love.

When you do that, you don't have to go out and find your fans. They're already there waiting for you.

STORYTELLING BEATS MARKETING

"When you go to bat as many times as I do, you're bound to get a good average."

—WALT DISNEY

When we first came to Savannah, we shared our message in the appropriate way, the way we were supposed to as a new baseball club. We marketed. We sold. We had other people carry our message while we tried to fit in. We failed. We failed because it wasn't compelling. It was just like everyone else's. It wasn't about people or an emotion or fun. It was about a product.

It wasn't until we brought the fans in and asked them to name the team that we turned things around. Finally, we had embraced not only the message but also the people who would tell it. In doing so, we went from marketers to something else: storytellers.

Attention beats marketing 1,000 percent of the time. While marketing will only get you so far, storytelling has no boundaries. The only limit is your own imagination.

PT Barnum knew this better than almost anyone. He was constantly writing and lecturing everywhere and anywhere—usually for free—spreading stories. Yes, a lot of his stories were fictionalized. While that worked for Barnum, the truth is you don't need fiction to make a good story.

Instead, just focus on the hero's journey. Good stories tell of challenges, adversity, and the struggle to succeed where everyone else failed. They tell of growth, transformation, and the quest to turn into something beautiful. They tell of leaders doing things no one else has tried in an attempt to make the world a better place.

Marketing "stories," on the other hand, only have one aim: to tell you how good a product or service is. That's short-term thinking. It's all about the quick win, the easy sale. But flash-in-the-pan marketing gets flash-in-the-pan results. Once people have bought from you, they'll quickly move on to the next transaction.

Stories focus on the long term. They're focused not on how good our product or service is but on how good our *people* are—us, our team, our fans. What we've done. What we've gone through. What we've become. The difference and impact we've made in people's lives. It's in these tales of transformation that we can create the biggest emotional gut punch—and sell out a couple of ballgames in a town two states over.

To tell a good story, think like a reporter. Define who you are, what you do, how you're different, what you're good at, and what you're all about. Along with the who, what, when, where, and why, think about the *meaning* of your business as well. What value would someone get out of your message? Why does it matter? Why is it worth sharing?

The point of playing reporter is to get yourself clear on your message. You could have a great story, but if you don't focus it, you could go overboard and talk too much. Remember, there is a point where people get tired of listening, so you have to be aware of that line. Is this still interesting? Is there still a point I need to make? A feeling I still need to get across? Questions like these will help strike that balance between when you may need to talk and when you may need to let the story find its own legs.

The ultimate goal is to create something so different, so unique, so unforgettable that everyone wants to share it with others. They buy in and own it; your message becomes their message. They become evangelists, speaking the word to anyone who will listen.

Say it with me now: share over sell. Serve over sell. Stories over sales. However you want to think about it, this is the key to spreading the love.

That Was Fun

"I've only had the pleasure of attending one Bananas game. My dad was a big baseball fan and had attended several games for the previous Savannah team. When he first heard the name Bananas, he didn't think much of it, but I tried to tell him it was going to be great. I even showed him videos of you running around town in a banana costume—he thought you were an idiot. On his weighty-first birthday, my brother and I took him to a Bananas game, and he loved it. His exact words were 'I don't know if we just saw a baseball game, a circus, or both—but that was fun!' A couple months later my dad was diagnosed with stage four cancer, and as he slowly lost his fight, his memories of the good times were what we talked about the most. My dad always talked about the time we all went to see 'that idiot in the yellow tuxedo run around during a baseball game.' He loved every minute. Thank you for all you do for families and the great game of baseball."

—BRIAN BAZEMORE, BANANAS FAN

WHAT'S YOUR FAN(TASY) STORY?

"Great stories happen to those who tell them."

—IRA GLASS

What do people want? They want to surround themselves with people who are passionate, who believe in something, who are committed to and energized by that passion so much they want to shout it from the rooftops.

Here's another key to spreading the love: you keep doing it. Once your story is out there, don't stop sharing. Always be passionate. Always be sharing.

Stories that continue to be shared evolve and grow. They're alive. Stories that stagnate die. People stop listening to them, and eventually they forget.

Luckily, there are plenty of avenues for storytelling. As I've mentioned throughout the book, social media and merch are major ways we share ours.

Whenever we release a new shirt, everyone on our staff gets one. We want them to feel more pride wearing the shirt than anyone else. Cody Carlee, our game-day teammate who works the merch store, has every jersey we've ever released. This begs the question: are your fans willing to wear your logo on a regular basis? Are they happy to wear your shirts when they don't have to? Are they proud to wear your logo in public? Not only that, but are they so proud they'll spread the word to their family and friends? Do they gift your merchandise to other people? Would they wear your merch even if they've never purchased or used your product or service?

Our superfans sure do. "I'm always proud wearing a Bananas shirt," Johnathan Walters says. "I play kickball on Sundays. There's not one day I've gone out there and someone's not wearing a Bananas hat or a Bananas shirt. Not one. It's really great knowing that you work for a company that people know. That's more humbling than anything."

Yes, it *is* humbling seeing people know who you are. And that they are proud to know you and want to spread your story. And when you see people sharing your story, you also know your business's story is healthy. Alive.

Storytelling, then, is a never-ending process. You can't just say, "Hey, we've got this." It's constantly looking at how to create unforgettable experiences and build that culture into your team.

Here's where things come full circle. The only way to build that culture into your team is to be a big fan of what you are doing. The biggest. If you love your creation that much, others will, too, and they will help you spread that creation—and spread that love.

When people see you doing something you love, they'll want to join your team. At the Bananas, we have the privilege of only hiring our fans, the people who love what we do as much as we do. They come to us. They want to help make us better. Some will even just volunteer their time and effort—like the Man-Nanas, the Banana Nanas, or our first pep band. Like many of our current employees. They just show up, each expressing some version of, "It's not about the money. I just want to be here."

That's what I want to encourage you to find. I'm not necessarily saying quit your job, but I do want you to find something that you're an absolute fan of, that gives you energy, that you'd do for free because it's really easy to go Fans First when you are doing what you love and want to share it with others.

No one wants to share a company or product they hate. No one will want to go Fans First for something that sucks the life out of them. You can't fake any of this. You can't fake belief, energy, or love—at least not for long. I see you always glancing at the clock. If you aren't losing track of time, you're doing the wrong thing.

Remember what I said back in part 1 of the book? You have to be a fanatic.

Fanatic has the same root word as *fan*. And when fanaticism is used to bring people joy, I see it as a good thing. It's what keeps that energy and drive up at four in the morning as you're closing down a show. It's what makes you write that bajillionth thank-you card. It's what keeps you wondering how to do a safe and family-friendly senior citizen lap dance in front of four thousand people. It's what you always think about on your runs—ten ideas a day, every morning, on what we're going to do next.

Why do I constantly think about the Bananas? And enjoy it? Because I'm a fan.

It's like the fans that follow the Grateful Dead, Dave Matthews, Phish, Lady Gaga. They plan whole seasons around following their idols around from concert to concert, helping out on set, meeting up with other fanatical fans, discussing setlists and the minute differences between performances. They don't want to miss a thing. And they are happy.

It bears repeating:
the first fan is you. Not your team.
Not your customers.
You.

Fulfillment is not about the money. It's about the love.

Maybe I'm just a crazy optimist, but I think everyone has the capacity to be fanatical—in a good way—about something they are passionate about. Many people have forgotten how to tap into that energy, that joy. As kids, we could tap into that child-like wonder all day. As adults, we've lost those happy thoughts and can no longer fly. If anything is ever going to help us remember that childlike wonder, I say it's stories.

It's All about Showing Up

Take a moment to create your fantasy career or company. What do you love so much you would show up for regardless of how much you got paid or how many hours you had to put in? What do you think is important, special, worth your free time? What gives you back that love?

STORIES ARE CONTAGIOUS

"You have to see it in person to truly understand. It is a temporary escape from reality with a baseball game going on in the background. Picture a perfect world where the food is free, the beer is cold, and the people are smiling. I know it sounds silly, but the weight of the world is left in the parking lot for a couple of hours."

—CHAT HOWARD, BANANAS FAN

As I set out to write this book, I asked our fans to share their Bananas stories. I got over a hundred fifty different stories. Fans whose stories I'd never heard. Fans from different time zones. Fans from different parts of the world. Coach Riley's mother sent me a four-thousand-word letter. Parts of many of those stories are in this book.

I'm not exactly sure what this response all means yet. I'm still processing. But I do know that our story has grown beyond us. I overhear fans all the time talking about us. Some call me the Willy Wonka of baseball. Some tell stories that veer hard into fiction (no, Banana Beard is not an outfielder on the team, and no, we don't have a *grandpa* senior citizen dance team). But as the fanbase grows, so does the legend.

It started with us shouting what we believed in from a mountaintop, and it's now in the hands of the fans. The journey has come full circle. They're the storytellers now.

How did our story grow to this level?

The interesting thing about those Grateful Dead, Phish, and Dave Matthews fanatics is that it's not just about the actual concert. It's also about the journey to the show, who they met, where they ate, and what mind-altering experience they had.

The story really isn't about the band. It's about them. The band only creates the stage the fan acts upon. It's the fans who write the script. They perform the show. They get the applause.

I'd like to think we've done the same. From eight-year-olds to eighty-year-olds, from interns to presidents, from far and near, we've given fans a chance to tell their own stories. Given them a stage to play out an experience. *They* are now the heroes. It's not about the Bananas—it never was. After all, it's not Bananas first. It's Fans First.

That's the one unifying thing about great stories: people can put themselves into them. They relate. They feel like they belong. Like they're a part of something bigger than themselves. And it's made their lives more meaningful and fulfilling.

As Darren Ross at Magic Castle Hotel said, "Stories are contagious." The greatest byproduct of a story is more stories. This is why it is so important to incentivize your team to create stories over sales. Whoever has the most stories wins. Whoever has the most epic story wins.

It doesn't matter where your stories come from—from you, from your First Fans, from your fans. The important thing is they come from the heart.

Whether you're telling a story or hearing a story for the first time, don't let that be the end of it. Listen to it. Share it. Embellish it. Collect it.

In our office, our storybook is as full of as many team and fans stories as we can collect. Imagine your own storybook. How many stories would you have at the end of each day, each week, each month?

Creating and collecting all those stories may sound exhausting in the macro, but it is the sum total of small daily efforts. It bears repeating: "Do for one what you wish you could do for many." Start with just one for one person. Do it and document it. You'll have your own book in no time.

Ultimately, the best way to create fans is to create stories. So get out there and start creating.

You Can Have My Tickets…and Come to Dinner

You've seen a lot of the ways we've spread our story through our own social media channels. But after your story becomes part of your fans' stories, they spread it in their own self-made and self-run channels.

On one of these channels, I came upon a fascinating discussion where a future fan was reaching out to our current fans for some information. The gentleman, who lived in Florida, had never been to a Bananas game, but he was writing a piece on us and wanted to know what we were all about.

What proceeded I can only describe as a game of kindness one-up-manship. There were glowing descriptions of the team. There were stories of amazing Fans First experiences. There were even tons of Bananas puns ("The talent makes the whole experience so "apeeling").

Then a few fans *really* got into it. One fan offered up four tickets to a game of the journalist's choosing: "You tell me what game you can make it up, and I'll give you my four tickets to enjoy! You will love it. We welcome you to Savannah!" Then another fan threw in a free dinner on top of that.

So why all this kindness? As another fan put it, "You would not be able to write about a Bananas experience if you haven't experienced it. You need to be there and get caught up in all the excitement." They were so invested in the journalist getting the story right that they removed every possible barrier to him actually attending a game in person!

THE LAST IMPRESSION

"Being the richest man in the cemetery doesn't matter to me. Going to bed at night saying we've done something wonderful—that's what matters to me."

—STEVE JOBS

In the book *Walt Disney's Way*, Andrew Lock shares a little-known story from Walt's life. Before he died, Walt Disney sent a letter to his friend, Art Linkletter. It included a photo of a small boy looking into the distance. Underneath the photo was a one-word caption: *priorities*. In the letter, Walt wrote, "A hundred years from now, it won't matter what's in your bank account or the kind of car you drive. It will only matter that you made a difference in the life of a child."

The priorities intrigue me. I keep thinking about the kids we've impacted, the stars of so many of the stories you've read in this book. There's something to be said about childlike wonder and passion, the impact something small can have on a life that's new and seeing the world for the first time. I want the first thing people see at a Bananas game to be wondrous, to bring back that childlike glee.

It's a longer game to play. That child grows up and has their own children. Then those children grow up and have their own children. After all that time has passed, will any of those children remember you?

In 2019, I had the privilege of reading our company's obituary. Or, maybe more accurately, our *It's a Wonderful Life* story, "What would happen if Fans First Entertainment didn't exist?" Here's what it said:

> Baseball died. It was a long, slow death. America's pastime stopped existing. Parents and grandparents could no longer share the game with their kids and grandkids. The game just became too slow, too boring, and too long to hold onto fans. Kids stopped playing baseball. Millions stopped going to ballparks and stopped watching on TV. Baseball became irrelevant in society.

Strong stuff. Now, what do we hope to happen because Fans First Entertainment *does* exist? Naturally, we wrote that out too.

> Fans First Entertainment saved baseball by creating a new game that was faster and filled with nonstop entertainment. It took the country by storm. Kids fell in love with this new game called Banana Ball. They began playing in the yard and emulating their favorite Banana Ballers. It seemed like a flashback to the 1950s and 1960s, when baseball was everything in our country. What started as a simple mantra, "We make baseball fun," turned into a new sport built solely on fun. It became known as the most fan-friendly sport in the world, and Fans First Entertainment became known as the most fan-centered company in the world. Overall, Fans First Entertainment serves as the gold standard for how to treat customers and employees. The concept of Fans First

took off with businesses worldwide. Customer experience and employee experience reached record highs of satisfaction, happiness, and engagement.

Just as businessman George Bailey learned in *It's a Wonderful Life,* it's the small acts that make the greatest changes, that ripple through not only our own lives but our kids' lives and their kids' lives—down through the generations.

Legacy is not what you leave for people; it's what you leave in people.

You never know how far your stories will go.

Even a small story creates a big ripple.

What kind of ripple are you creating? What would happen if your business never existed? What *can* happen because it does? How many lives can you change while you're here?

If your answers to these questions are *nothing* and *no one*, then something needs to change.

And it starts by changing the life of a single person.

The Bananas Bookshelf

Fanocracy: Turning Fans into Customers and Customers into Fans by David Meerman Scott and Reiko Scott

Monster Loyalty by Lady Gaga

GO BANANAS!

"All of our dreams can come true if we have the courage to pursue them."

—WALT DISNEY

The first time I went to do something a little crazy and fun with my then-two-and-a-half-year-old son, he wouldn't do it.

I had the bright idea to take Maverick to a trampoline park. I thought it was a bright idea, anyway. But he was terrified—so much so that he wouldn't even go inside at first.

Finally, I coaxed him in. Then I coaxed him to take off his shoes. He sat in the lobby and looked at everyone jumping for a full thirty minutes. Then, once he was finally *on* a trampoline, he sat down cross-legged and was too afraid to jump.

I snapped a photo of him and texted it to Emily. "This is going well," it said.

Finally, Maverick slowly stood up and held onto my hands.

He moved a little bit.

Then he moved a little bit more.

Then a smile blossomed across his face, and he started jumping.

A few months later, three-year-old Maverick *owned* the trampoline park. He was all about getting air, going wild, not knowing when he'd come down. "Daddy, look! Daddy, look!" he screamed as he reached for new heights.

So what's the lesson here?

It's only scary because you've never done it. And it's never as scary as you thought it would be once you do it.

And the truth of the matter is, there's always something you haven't done.

Every time I'm about to do something new, I'm scared to do it just like anyone else. I was scared when we first came to Savannah. I was scared to unveil Banana Ball to an unsuspecting world. I was scared when we launched the One City World Tour.

I was even scared to wear my yellow tux to the airport when I flew to give speeches. What would people think? Would I end up on social media, being mocked for looking so cartoonishly awkward and out of place?

Considering that one of my deepest fears is to be misrepresented, the idea of something happening like this was awful. But my fear of appearing at a speaking gig with a luggage-wrinkled tux was bigger. So I made the leap.

As you saw with Maverick, overcoming fear comes in steps. The first time I wore a yellow tux, I was at my home stadium—my turf, my script, my context. I got comfortable with it.

Then I started wearing the tux during speaking gigs. I was in a new environment, albeit one where I could still control people's perception of me.

Then I started wearing the tux on the way to my speaking gigs. A lot less control there. Same for when I started wearing the tux out to meals after the gigs. Now I had no control. I stood out like, well, a ripe banana.

Each was a new step where I felt a little bit more comfortable. That's the progression.

That's why it's such a big deal to fans at Bananas games with their banana-themed accessories, their banana-shaped beards, and their banana tattoos. When they're at the show, they know they have nothing to be afraid of. From there, they can learn to push past other boundaries in whatever way they're uncomfortable with.

Every day they show up, they're building up more courage to live bold and loud, to step out into the world—not the way they're expected to be but the way they *want* to be.

I now wear my tux to the airport when I need to. The third or fourth time I was flying in my tux, I had a layover in Indianapolis. As I hopped on the escalator and began to ride up, a gentleman heading the opposite direction looked at me and yelled, "Go Bananas!"

Once you make the leap, it's never as bad as it seems.

Being a fan is all about moments like these. When you're a fan, you're always a moment away from seeing and connecting with another fan. Fandom creates belonging. It makes people feel like they matter—and, as I've said before, nothing matters more than making people feel like they matter.

This last part may be scary, so remember what I just told you.

You can't be corporate first, profits first, or shareholders first and still be Fans First. Sorry, but that's not how the word *first* works.

By choosing Fans First, you *are* breaking the rules. Rules hold you back. They make you feel bad about your choices. They create friction. They tell you to *not* entertain, to *not* experiment, to *not* empower, and to *not* engage. They zap your energy.

Let the Five Es be your bat to break the rules. They're rules to break rules. Maybe they're the only rules you should have. And as you swing that bat, remember: swing hard in case you hit it.

The first time Maverick and I took swings in the backyard, he missed five in a row. I said to him, "The more you take, the more you make." He swung and missed a few more times. But when he finally hit a line drive, he broke out in a smile as wide as Grayson Stadium. Now, in any situation, after I say, "The more you take," he says, "The more you make."

He knows what's most important.

After you swing hard, swing again. Keep swinging hard, even if you miss—just in case you hit it.

Stand out. Have fun. Create fans.

It's your turn now. Go Bananas!

STAND BY ME

"Our goal is to go out like Willie Nelson—on a high."

—TED LASSO

It's 9:55 p.m. I'm standing out in front of the gate of Grayson Stadium surrounded by hundreds of fans. The last game of the 2021 season is over. The Bananas are CPL champions once again, and no one wants to leave.

The Bananas staff is lined up on both sides of the gate, thanking fans. The Banana Band is playing as the fans continue to make their way outside the stadium.

The players are spread out, singing, dancing, signing autographs, and taking pictures. Split and the Man-Nanas are doing the same. A few minutes prior, I was actually asked to sign a gentleman's backside. Well, his underwear, to be exact. Except he was wearing it. Even though this was a first, I knew quickly why I was being asked. This was the person I'd thrown the Dolce & Banana underwear to earlier in the game.

Everything happening around me is so surreal, I can't help but smile and laugh at it all.

Then Bill LeRoy starts ballroom dancing with a nine-year-old girl. Her name is Hannah. She's wearing a pink T-shirt, and it's her birthday. Bill twirls Hannah around, doing underarm turns and dips, carefully maintaining a friendly dance hold as he leads her through the steps, her mother recording the moment to post to her TikTok later.

Split and the rest of the players form a semi-circle around their dance space. Time to make the moment even more special. They start singing "Happy Birthday," followed by an impromptu hip-hop remix from one of the other players.

At that moment, I hear the band start singing. It's the opening bars to the all-time classic "Stand by Me."

Almost one by one, I watch the players join in to sing. They link their arms together and start swaying as a group. Then Split, the staff, the coaches, the Man-Nanas, and the couple hundred fans that stayed till the end all follow suit. Bill and Hannah are still twirling. They've all come together.

Bill thanks his dance partner. Hannah grins. The remaining fans cheer in unison.

It's a magical moment—one of the most magical moments we have. Every night after every game, I think about what this plaza party means.

All around us are people from different backgrounds and different home states, mingling with different players, cast members, musicians, fans. And we're all standing together.

This is why we do what we do. It's to bring people together, to bring them joy, happiness, and fun. But it's also to bring them family—a Banana family.

That's how a night in Bananaland finishes: players, staff, characters, and fans all together with our arms around each other singing "Stand by Me."

It's so simple and easy, but you can't beat that for a last impression.

THANK YOU

As we finish this book, I am overcome with gratitude for everyone who made this happen.

Since starting the Savannah Bananas with Emily, I've had big dreams for this team. Never in those dreams did I envision writing a book about all the magical memories and amazing lessons I've learned along the way.

But Banana Nation made this happen. This tribe of supporters has become larger than I ever imagined and deserves all the credit for this book.

You have been growing with us since day 1, supporting us in anything we do or try with the team. From naming the team after a fruit to introducing new crazy characters every season at the ballpark to even creating the new game of Banana Ball, you've encouraged us to keep entertaining and keep making baseball fun.

Your support grew stronger with this book. So many of you sent in title ideas and stories of your experiences with the team— and you even helped pick out the cover. Many of you have sent in notes of encouragement and praise. Writing a book can be a lonely project, but you made it feel like we were doing this together, which meant the world to me.

Next, the biggest Bananas fans, our team members who make the magic happen day in and day out in Savannah and all over the world on our Banana Ball Tour. For this book, you told me numerous stories that I had never heard and shared memories that helped make this book what it is today. You are the ones who live Fans First every day. You bring the joy and the fun to the fans and to everyone in the office. You make me truly proud of what we've built and the impact we are making.

For the OG Bananas who have been with us since that first season: President Jared Orton, Marie Matzinger, Patrick Briody, Berry Aldridge, and Lizzy Mackerty. You've built the foundation for Fans First and everything that has been shared in this book. I have so much love for all of you!

For the team at Scribe who worked with me on this project for almost two years. Tucker Max for helping work through the ideas to involve the fans and share the process. Kacy Wren for being with me every step of the way on the process and deadlines.

Also from Scribe, my editor Chas Hoppe. To say you are a legend is an understatement. After writing my first book, *Find Your Yellow Tux*, with you, it was a no-brainer to team up again for this second book. However, we both never knew how challenging this round was going to be. With so many new voices and stories, transcripts, and interviews to go through, the effort you put in was second to none. From helping rewrite the entire first part of the book to having me send ten pages of revisions after the first manuscript, you embraced the challenge and stayed positive through it all. You encouraged me to continue to have fun and added so many unique and Bananas-like elements to the book that made it what it is today.

Next, to all the groups, businesses, and conferences that have booked me to speak. The Five Es and many of the elements of this book were tested in front of you all and proved to me that they were worth sharing in written form. To Li Hayes, my amazing speaking coordinator, thank you for being my biggest cheerleader and supporter of our Fans First mission.

To my dad, even today, I'm still just that five-year-old kid coming to bat and swinging hard trying to make you proud. Dad, you've encouraged me every step along the way and pushed me to work hard and stay positive with everything I do. I love you, Dad, and I hope I made you proud with this book.

To my kids, thank you for the lessons you taught me as I wrote this book. Maverick, seeing you overcome obstacles and your fears inspires me daily to tackle new adventures. Seeing you guys fall down but get back up encourages me to keep swinging and trying new things. Hearing you say, "The more you take, the more you make," fires me up and motivates me to do the same.

Finally, my wife, Emily. When we got married in the rain at the stadium, I'm not sure if you knew everything you were signing up for. But from that day on, we've learned to roll with anything that came our way. You've been the rock for me and our family that pushes us onward through all adversity and challenges.

You've taught me to be present and live in the moment. Through it all, your amazing gratitude has led the way.

Every night before Emily and I go to sleep, we finish with an exercise we call "Rose, Rose, Bud." It's a simple practice where we share two great things that happened during the day and one thing that we are looking forward to in the upcoming day.

This ritual has helped us finish every day with gratitude. Most importantly, it has taught us to always look for the good and see the beautiful things in the day.

In *Find Your Yellow Tux,* I shared how I start every day by writing a thank-you letter. I believe how you finish the day is just as important.

To close out this section and the book, my final rose is for you, the reader. I am truly grateful to you for making it this far in this book. In all seriousness, your investment of time and energy into hearing about Fans First means so much to me. We have a strong vision to bring Fans First to the world and thank you for being there with us on this journey.

As gratitude is meant to be shared, I'll leave you by asking what your roses are today and who you can share them with.

Thanks again for everything, and Go Bananas!

Oh, and one more thing...

PLUS EVERYTHING

"The way I see it, Disneyland will never be finished. It's something that we can keep developing and adding to. Motion picture is different. Once it's wrapped up and sent out to processing, we're through with it. If there are things that could be improved, we can't do anything about them anymore. I've always wanted to work on something alive, something that keeps growing. We've got that in Disneyland."

—WALT DISNEY

"So, uh, do you have any advice or suggestions on how to throw this?"

I'm standing next to Jake Peavy. National League Cy Young award-winner Jake Peavy. Two-time World Series champion Jake Peavy. One of the all-time great pitchers in baseball. *That* Jake Peavy.

And he's asking me for pitching advice.

After all, he's never thrown out a banana before.

No one has when we ask them to throw out the First Banana. From ballplayers like Jake to mayors, famous authors, grandmas, and kids, most of them respond the same way: amused by what they're about to do—and confused about how to actually do it.

Jake is a good sport about the whole thing, though. And he knows how much it means for him, Mobile's hometown hero, to make an appearance at the show. He didn't quite know what we meant when we asked him to throw out the First Banana, but he said he'd be happy to do it anyway.

Now here we are in the tunnel at Hank Aaron Stadium, and I'm giving him pitching advice.

"Well, Jake, you just drop your elbow and make sure you get it there," I say. Unlike the majority of our First Banana pitchers, I've had a lot of practice at this. Then I add, "Throw a strike or they'll boo you," mimicking what Derek Jeter told George W. Bush before the then-president threw out the first pitch after the events of September 11, 2001.

"All right," he says with a smile. "I'll do my best." And with that, Jake Peavy trots out to the mound, and I grab the mic to announce him.

"Fans, please welcome to the field Mobile native, Cy Young Award-winner, and World Series champion Jake Peavy!"

After a big ovation and a few obligatory pics, it's Jake's time to shine.

He throws a perfect strike. Right down the middle.

The crowd goes wild.

Jake smiles, tips his cap to the crowd, and heads back off the field.

"Thanks again for doing this, Jake. That was really special," I tell him.

"Anything for the fans," he says.

My thoughts exactly—especially if that means giving the fans a little extra. After all, why throw out a first pitch when you can throw out a First Banana? Why end a book after the conclusion when you could throw in one more chapter for good measure?

That's right, folks: this chapter is all about plussing.

Fans First Firsts

"My son, Jack Weeks, threw out the First Banana at the first-ever Savannah Bananas game way back when. You randomly picked him out of the crowd, and he threw the banana over home plate for a perfect strike. He kept his banana trophy on his chest of drawers for about two years after this."

—STEPHEN WEEKS, BANANAS FAN

WHAT IS PLUSSING?

"From the usher to the field crew to the players to the ownership, we want that fan to have the best experience they can. Nobody leaves disappointed."

—MARTY JONES

It was 1959, and Disneyland had just received a $6 million-dollar expansion of Tomorrowland, including a monorail and new rides like Space Mountain and the Matterhorn. The investment immediately paid off, with attendance hitting a new record high that same year.

But Walt wasn't ready to rest on his laurels. Next, he wanted to spend another $350,000 on a Christmas parade.

You could almost hear his accountants and managers spitting out their coffee in unison. "You want to spend $350,000 dollars for a *parade?* What's the point? The guests are already going to be there. Disneyland is already going to have their money. No one's expecting a parade, so why even bother?"

Walt heard their protests, but he politely waved them off. "We should do the parade precisely because no one is expecting it," Walt said. "We can't be satisfied, even though we'll get the crowds at Christmas. We've always got to give them a little bit more. It will be worth the investment. If they ever stop coming, it will cost us ten times that much to get them back."

In *Built to Last,* author Jim Collins says the critical question visionary companies ask themselves is, "How can we do better tomorrow than we did today?" This question becomes a way of life. There is no ultimate finish line for a visionary company. There is no "having made it." Visionary companies are terribly demanding of themselves. Six decades later, and Disneyland and the Walt Disney Company have more raving fans than ever. And it's not just because they produce great movies, shows, and rides. That's part of it. But the other part is that they're committed to giving their fans new experiences, moments they don't expect, moments that will thrill and delight them.

That's what plussing is all about.

Plussing means giving your fans more than what they paid for, more than what they expect, sometimes even more than it seems reasonable to do.

To plus something is to improve it—but not in the normal, boring, "How can we make this a teeny bit better next time?" sense. It's about going big, about mixing in the familiar with the unexpected. That way, you don't just trigger old, happy memories—you create *new ones.*

This is the special kind of alchemy that makes a $350,000 Christmas parade a safe bet. By plussing the experience at every point, your fans feel seen, heard, and understood. They know you're not there just to take their money but to give them an unforgettable experience. If you truly want to go Fans First, then you've got to be plussing every moment.

FIVE WAYS TO PLUS YOUR BUSINESS

"Most teams see the opening day as the finish line. They get to the opening day. Everything is ready, and now we cruise through the season. Nothing has a finish line. Nothing is done. How can it be better? How can it be plussed? I believe the next game will always be the best experience that we've ever put on. Tomorrow night will be the best experience. I'm not saying last night was the worst experience, but it had better be better the next night."

—JARED ORTON, BANANAS PRESIDENT

In the book *Simple Truths of Service*, Ken Blanchard and Barbara Glanz tell the story of Johnny, a bagger at a local grocery store. One day, a consultant came to the store and encouraged every member to think of how they could add their "service signature" to their work—in other words, how they could plus the customer experience.

For Johnny's service signature, he decided to share "Johnny's Thoughts," little slips of paper with observations and positive affirmations that he would add to each customer's grocery bags as they were checking out. The idea was an instant hit. Customers would get their groceries, head out to their cars, discover the thought Johnny had included, and start smiling.

Then a funny thing happened: Johnny's checkout line became the hottest line in the grocery store. It didn't matter that there were other checkout lines open. The customers wanted Johnny's thoughts, and they were willing to wait a little extra to get them. They were also willing to make return trips, with many customers upping their visits from once a week to two or three times a week. Such was the power of plussing.

Seeing Johnny's success, the other employees at the store began adding their own service signatures. The florist started handing out extra flowers to grandmas and little girls (which is such a good idea that we started doing it too). Then, the deli started coordinating fun sticker-related activities with other departments in the store. Eventually, everyone and every department had their own signature service, just like Johnny.

There is a key lesson here about plussing: you can't force your team to plus. They have to see the value, come to it on their own, and then make it their own. If you can unlock that feeling, then your team will walk around the workplace in an entirely new way. Everywhere they look, they'll ask, "How can I plus this? What's one new touchpoint I can add here? How can I invest a little more to plus the fan experience?"

A culture of plussing has been the key to the Bananas' success. It's what keeps us energetic, engaged, and, most importantly, relevant. It's what makes all our shenanigans matter, too, because it's these plussing moments that people remember most of all. Here are five plussing practices we use to keep the ideas flowing.

1. Get in Your Fans' Shoes

Not long before he died, Walt Disney said, "Whenever I go on a ride, I always ask, 'What's wrong with this thing? How can it be improved?'" In other words, he put himself in his guests' shoes and figured out how he could improve their experience.

The reason we do the Undercover Fan every single night is because we want to park, walk in, sit, and eat not only with the fans but like a fan. We want to feel all the frustrations and friction points. Everything that a fan would notice, we want to notice—because it's those little things they'll tell their friends and family about.

2. Go Where Your Fans Are

If you want to plus an experience, don't plus it from your office, boardroom, conference room, or house. Plus it from where your customers experience it. This includes online and call-in spaces as well as physical ones.

3. Shorten the Feedback Loop

Many companies have annual or quarterly reviews. We have daily reviews designed to sharpen our fan experience. First, we go over the pros and grows for the night from our Undercover Fan. Then, Director of Entertainment Zack Frongillo and I do laps around the field, where we talk about all the areas that we can improve and how we can get better. Finally, once we've gone over all of that, we start brainstorming ways to not only improve those experiences but to plus them.

4. Bring in Outsiders

We're proud of what we do. Sometimes, we might be too proud. Because we've figured out so much on our own and because we have such a unique way of looking at things, we've always been a little reluctant to bring in outside consultants.

But if you're committed to plussing, then you've got to be honest with yourself on your strengths and weaknesses. We're great at putting on a show, but we're still figuring out areas like staffing and food and beverage operations. Bringing in experts in these areas has helped us to see blind spots more quickly and comprehensively than we ever could have done on our own.

Every time a consultant comes to the ballpark, it's all but guaranteed one or more of us will exclaim, "Huh, that's so obvious now that you mention it. Why didn't we think of that?" Of course, once the experts have had their say, then we set about not only addressing our blind spots but plussing them.

5. Go Deep in One Area

You can plus every aspect of your business. But you can't plus every aspect of your business in one day. For the Bananas, there are so many different directions we could go, from first impressions to last impressions, from the show to concessions, from ticketing to merchandise. Everything helps, but we always try to focus on the area that needs our attention the most.

These areas change over time. In the beginning, we focused on plussing the show. Baseball was long, slow, and boring, and we wanted our fans to know we were doing something different. In 2021, we went deep on our pregame show. A lot of fans arrive at our ballpark as much as two hours before the First Banana, and we don't want them to be bored for a second.

6. Know What Business You're In

Did I say there were only five ways to plus your business? Oh well. Here's an extra one.

We play baseball, but we're not in the baseball business. We're in the entertainment business. Once we made that distinction, we gave ourselves permission to be more than a baseball team. That has made all the difference in creating an unforgettable experience.

THE ART OF "WHAT IF?"

"A revolution starts with a clear vision of a world different than the one we live in today."

—SIMON SINEK

If you were to simplify the Bananas' process to its essential ingredients, it would all come down to a single question: "What if?"

This is the most powerful question I can think of—and it lies at the core of a plussing mindset. "What if?" can turn the most ho-hum, run-of-the-mill experience into something completely new. All you have to do is ask how things could be different.

For a while, we'd been plussing the postgame experience with our Party in the Plaza. The band played, the players sang and signed autographs, and everyone intermingled and had a great time. One day, however, we realized that another group of fans, the fans who left early—didn't get anything more than a wave and a thank you. Where was the plus in that?

As soon as we realized the problem, we set about brainstorming ideas. That was when the what-ifs came in:

- What if we got a bubble machine and had the fans walk through a tunnel of bubbles in order to leave? (Fun, but not good enough.)

- What if we got a mariachi band to follow fans out and serenade them all the way to their cars? (How could we possibly hire enough mariachi bands to follow every single fan out?)

- What if we had a mysterious gatekeeper who appeared in a cloak and asked fans a series of banana-related riddles before they were allowed to leave? (Too ominous, not enough fun.)

Some of those were pretty fun ideas, and we might even do them some day. But ultimately, we settled on s'mores—because who doesn't love s'mores? As the fans walked out the gates, we'd be there at the ready with our little fire canisters, our chocolate, our grahams, and our marshmallows on sticks.

The idea was a big plus, but the experience came with some minuses too. For one thing, we were in a small space and could only serve ten people at a time. For another, it was extremely messy (marshmallow goo does *not* clean easily). The fans loved the idea of it, but the sticky fingers before they got in their cars didn't exactly leave them thrilled.

Eventually, we had to face the truth: fresh s'mores served up in the sweaty Savannah summer wasn't the plus we thought it would be. Instead of adding to the experience, we were just creating another friction point.

Still, we knew the basic idea was good, so we started brainstorming ideas that weren't so messy. What could bring fans joy like s'mores did but that wouldn't be so messy?

Then the answer hit me like a moonbeam. Actually, more like a MoonPie.

After a game, our Grandma Coach, Marty Barrington, handed me a banana MoonPie. My eyes instantly lit up. I hadn't had one of these in years. This would be a perfect replacement for our s'mores!

As soon as we could get our hands on enough MoonPies, we were out at the exit once again, handing every fan a little blast from their childhood, complete with a zinger of a pun to go with it: "We're over the moon you came out here tonight!" "This pie is bananas!" Are the jokes a little cheesy? You'd better believe it. But hey, you gotta plus the plus.

With "What if?" as our guide, we discovered how to plus the fan experience for an overlooked and unseen part of our crowd: the early birds. The MoonPies aren't much (unless you're buying them in bulk), but they're another way to bring joy, happiness, and fun and to make even the fans who leave early feel like family.

Plussing takes practice. Sometimes it's downright messy. But it's the core mindset that brings the Fans First Way to life. Commit to trying something new every day, and test the results. Then, add a little bit more every time you do it—really push yourself. It's not going to work every time, but if you're constantly dancing on the edge of calamity, that means you're probably doing it right.

If you treat every day like a game day, no matter what business you are in, you're sure to win.

Okay, now we're done for real this time. Or at least, the book is. Your journey is just getting started.

Time to stand out, have fun, and start creating some fans!

JOIN THE FANS FIRST MOVEMENT

We love to hear from our fans. Here are some ways to stay engaged with us!

Bananas on the Web: www.savannahbananas.com

Bananas on social media:

- **TikTok:** @thesavbananas

- **Instagram:** @thesavbananas

- **Twitter:** @TheSavBananas

- **Facebook:** https://www.facebook.com/TheSavBananas

- **YouTube:** TheSavannahBananas

Bananas mini-documentary: Savannah Bananas Story on YouTube.

Bananaphone:

- To hear the best hold music ever, call us at Bananas Global Headquarters: 912-712-2482.

- If you have a question or want to share a takeaway from the book, drop Jesse a text: 781-424-2499.

ABOUT THE AUTHOR

Jesse Cole is a fanatic about fandom. In 2016, he founded Fans First Entertainment and launched the Savannah Bananas with one mission: to spark a fan-focused movement. Whether at the ballpark, on social media, onstage delivering keynotes, in features for ESPN and *Entrepreneur*, or in his first book, *Find Your Yellow Tux*, Jesse continues to create fans all over the world.

Jesse is the proud inventor of Banana Ball and Dolce & Banana underwear and not-so-proud promoter of the Human Horse Race and Flatulence Fun Night. He's a raving fan of his wife Emily, his kids, and peerless promoters like Walt Disney, PT Barnum, and Bill Veeck. Jesse owns seven yellow tuxedos.